OMS

Lessons Learned

Model Early Foreign Language Programs

Printed in the United States of America
10 9 8 7 6 5 4 3 2 1

Professional Practice Series 1

Editorial/production supervision: Jeanne Rennie
Copyediting: Jeanne Rennie
Editorial/production/design assistance: Sonia Kundert
Design and cover: SAGARTdesign

ISBN 1-887744-63-0

Prepared for publication by the ERIC Clearinghouse on Languages and Linguistics and the Northeast and Islands Regional Educational Laboratory At Brown University. Published by the Center for Applied Linguistics and Delta Systems Co, Inc.

Funding for the research and information collection that led to the development of this publication was provided by the following:

U.S. Department of Education
Office of Postsecondary Education
International Research and Studies Program
Grant No. PO17A50054

U.S. Department of Education
Office of Educational Research
and Improvement
Contract No. RJ96006401

Funding for development and production of the book itself was provided by the following:

U.S. Department of Education
Office of Educational Research and Improvement
National Library of Education
Contract No. ED-99-CO-0008

The opinions expressed in this publication are those of the authors and do not necessarily reflect the positions or policies of any office of the U.S. Department of Education.

Library of Congress Cataloging-in-Publication Data
Gilzow, Douglas F.
  Lessons learned : model early foreign language programs / Douglas F. Gilzow,
Lucinda E. Branaman.
    p. cm.
  "Prepared for publication by the ERIC Clearinghouse on Languages and Linguistics
and by the Northeast and Islands Regional Educational Laboratory at Brown
University."
  Includes bibliographical references.
  ISBN 1-887744-63-0 (pbk.)
  1. Language and languages--Study and teaching--United States. I. Branaman,
Lucinda E. II. ERIC Clearinghouse on Languages and Linguistics. III. Northeast and
Islands Regional Educational Laboratory at Brown University. IV. Title.
  P57.U5 G55 2000
  372.65'044'0973--dc21   00-064502

Lessons Learned
Model Early Foreign Language Programs

Douglas F. Gilzow
Lucinda E. Branaman

CAL
Center for Applied Linguistics

CAL's mission is to improve communication through better understanding of language and culture. CAL's staff of educators and researchers are dedicated to promoting and improving the teaching and learning of languages, identifying and solving problems related to language and culture, and serving as a resource for information about language and culture. CAL's activities include research, teacher education, analysis and dissemination of information, development of instructional materials and language assessments, technical assistance, program evaluation, and policy analysis. CAL is a private, non-profit organization.

ERIC®
Educational Resources Information Center
Clearinghouse on Languages & Linguistics
(ERIC/CLL)

ERIC is a nationwide information network that aims to improve educational practice by providing ready access to current education literature. ERIC maintains the world's largest database of education-related materials, operates extensive question-answering services covering all subject areas and levels of education, and produces and distributes a wide range of publications designed to provide easy access to important information on topics in education. ERIC clearinghouses collect, produce, and disseminate education information in various subject areas. ERIC/CLL's subject area includes foreign language education, the teaching and learning of English as a second language, bilingual education, and all areas of linguistics. ERIC/CLL is operated by the Center for Applied Linguistics through a contract from the U.S. Department of Education, Office of Educational Research and Improvement, National Library of Education.

L A B

Northeast And Islands Regional Educational Laboratory At Brown University

The LAB is one in a network of ten regional laboratories funded by the Office of Educational Research and Improvement of the U.S. Department of Education. The LAB collaborates with researchers, schools, and communities to promote systemic school improvement in Connecticut, Maine, Massachusetts, New Hampshire, New York, Rhode Island, Vermont, Puerto Rico, and the Virgin Islands. Knowledge gained through inquiries into standards and assessment, school services, professional development, and community involvement is exchanged with policymakers and schools through publications, computer media, and LAB-facilitated workshops. The LAB is a program of the Education Alliance at Brown University. The Center for Applied Linguistics partners with the LAB on projects in language and cultural diversity.

Delta Systems Co., Inc.
Bringing Language to the World

Delta Systems Co., Inc. is a publisher and distributor of ESL and foreign language materials. Since 1993, Delta has had a co-publishing agreement with the Center for Applied Linguistics. Joint CAL/Delta publications include the *Language in Education: Theory and Practice* series of professional reference books and the *Topics in Immigrant Education* series. Delta and CAL's most recent joint venture is the *Professional Practice Series,* of which this book is the first volume.

Contents

continued

The Professional Practice Series

Like almost everyone else in today's fast-paced world, teachers and education administrators are very busy people. In addition to working with students in the classroom and designing and overseeing educational programs, they are likely to be involved in curriculum development; design and development of instructional materials; committee assignments; coordination of after-school activities; and communication with parents, counselors, community leaders, and others involved in the education of their students. In addition, they need to stay abreast of new research and developments in their subject areas and in the field of education. Reading the literature, attending conferences, and participating in and leading workshops and in-service training sessions are all part of their ongoing professional development.

Teachers and administrators need ready access to clear and reliable information about effective practices in language education. The *Professional Practice Series,* developed by the ERIC Clearinghouse on Languages and Linguistics and published by the Center for Applied Linguistics and Delta Systems, is designed to provide practitioners with current information on topics, trends, and techniques in language teaching. Each volume begins with an overview of the topic and the chapters in the book. Each chapter focuses on a particular program, practice, or practitioner that has been shown to be successful. The chapters describe the strategies and techniques used by effective teachers and administrators and offer practical guidelines and suggestions to help others implement similar strategies in their own classrooms, schools, and districts. Each volume closes with a summary of key points in the book and general guidelines and recommendations.

It is our hope that the *Professional Practice Series* will provide language educators with accessible, timely information, supported by theory and research, that will help them improve or enhance their teaching and their programs.

Jeanne Rennie and Joy Kreeft Peyton, Series Editors
Center for Applied Linguistics
Washington, DC

For online information about this series and other books included in it, visit www.practiceseries.com.

Acknowledgments

The authors offer their deepest appreciation to all the teachers, administrators, parents, and students who shared information about their programs with us so that it could be shared with others.

Special thanks and recognition go to Jennifer Locke, who, with co-author Lucinda Branaman, traveled to model programs, visited classes, and interviewed numerous teachers, parents, students, and program administrators.

Thanks also go to the experts from the National Network for Early Language Learning (NNELL) who served on the program selection panel: Penny Armstrong, Pittsburg (Kansas) Community Schools; Audrey Heining-Boynton, University of North Carolina–Chapel Hill; and Marcia Rosenbusch, Iowa State University.

We would also like to thank our colleagues at the Northeast and Islands Regional Educational Laboratory At Brown University, especially Mary-Beth Fafard and Thomas Crochunis, who have provided encouragement and support to the model programs project.

At the Center for Applied Linguistics, Donna Christian, Carolyn Temple Adger, Annette Holmes, Liz Howard, and Chris Montone provided substantial support to the project, especially in the data collection phase. Nancy Rhodes, model programs project director, and Joy

Kreeft Peyton, director of the ERIC Clearinghouse on Languages and Linguistics, provided ongoing support and guidance at every step, from project design to preparation for publication. Jeanne Rennie edited the final manuscript and expertly shepherded it through the publication process. Vincent Sagart designed the cover and the interior of the book, and Sonia Kundert ably assisted in all aspects of its production.

Introduction

This is an exciting time in the field of early foreign language education in the United States. A recent survey indicates that 31% of elementary schools are offering foreign language instruction, up from 22% a decade ago (Rhodes & Branaman, 1999). National standards for K–12 foreign language education are now helping to guide instruction, assessment, and teacher preparation. The number and variety of early foreign language programs are growing, giving students new opportunities to gain proficiency in a second language.

As parents and educators become more aware of the benefits of early language learning, they are increasingly seeking information on how to establish language programs in their own school or district. They need information in areas as diverse as funding; advocacy and public relations; curriculum and materials; evaluation and assessment; and teacher qualifications, preparation, and certification. *Lessons Learned* aims to address these information needs by describing seven successful early foreign language programs. It is hoped that these programs will serve as models from which others can draw information and ideas for developing their own programs.

All of the programs described in this book are early-start, long-sequence programs that start in preschool or the elementary grades and continue through high school, and all have been in operation for at least 4 years. But each is unique. Some are in stable, middle-class neighborhoods; others are in far more fluid or less affluent communities. Several receive funding through federal or state grant programs, whereas others are supported entirely by local district funds. The amount of foreign language instruction children receive in these programs varies from a few lessons each week to half of every school day. Some programs offer only one foreign language; others offer four or five. But in all seven programs, children are learning to understand and communicate in a new language.

Selecting the Seven Programs

The seven foreign language programs described in this book were identified through a nomination and selection process informed by national standards for foreign language education and by research on effective language instruction for elementary and middle school students (Curtain & Pesola, 1994; National Standards in Foreign Language Education Project, 1996). The programs selected met the following criteria:

- Curricula based on the "five Cs"of the national foreign language standards—communication, cultures, connections, comparisons, and communities
- Regular program evaluation
- Outcomes that meet program goals
- Accessibility for all students
- Communication and coordination across content areas
- A student population that reflects the ethnic and socioeconomic diversity of the local population
- Articulation from elementary to middle school and from middle school to high school
- Professional development for teachers
- Support from the community

In addition, programs had to be at least 4 years old and willing to share their curricula with other programs. (See Appendix 1 for a fuller description of the selection and information-gathering process for this project).

Naturally, the seven programs vary in how fully they exemplify any one of these attributes. It is important to note that these are *model* programs, not *dream* programs. As the program implementers themselves would agree, none is perfect. Each of these programs has faced the kind of challenges typically encountered by innovative educational programs: Budgets are cut, grants expire, and skeptical administrators question the value of the program. At the same time, federal and state governments are demanding greater accountability and adherence to ambitious standards that may not have been anticipated in original program plans. Staff in the seven model programs described in this book know these and other problems very well. They have had to find and keep qualified teachers, develop practical and reliable assessment procedures, and generate or maintain community-wide support for the idea of foreign language instruction in the early grades. The staffs of these seven model programs have addressed these challenges in creative ways, as will be seen in the following chapters.

The Seven Model Programs

The seven model programs include five content-enriched FLES programs, one partial immersion program, and one middle school immersion continuation program. "Content-enriched" programs are those in which language lessons include concepts from subjects such as math, science, or geography, mostly as reinforcement of subject matter classes taught in English. In this book, "content-based" refers to programs in which students take a subject such as science, mathematics, or social studies in the foreign language. The French immersion program in Prince George's County, Maryland, for example, is a content-based program.

One of the seven programs is located in the west/southwest, two in the southeast, one in the mid-Atlantic, one in the midwest, and two in the northeast. (See 1.01, next page.) The schools visited in these programs taught Spanish, French, Japanese, and Russian. Other languages, such as German and Chinese, are taught at some program schools but not at those visited by project researchers. Grade levels range from kindergarten through Grade 8. Three of the programs exist at a single school, the other four are district-wide programs.

1.01 ■

	NORTHEAST	MID-ATLANTIC	SOUTHEAST	MIDWEST/ CENTRAL	WEST/ SOUTHWEST
CONTENT-ENRICHED FLES	Springfield Public Schools, MA (Chinese, French, Russian, and Spanish) Glastonbury Public Schools, CT (French, Japanese, Russian, Spanish)		Bay Point Elementary School, Pinellas County Schools, FL (Spanish) Ephesus Road Elementary School, Chapel Hill-Carrboro Public Schools, NC (French)	Larchmont Elementary School, Toledo Public Schools, OH (Spanish)	
PARTIAL IMMERSION					Richmond Elementary School, Portland Public Schools, OR (Japanese)
MIDDLE SCHOOL IMMERSION CONTINUATION		Andrew Jackson and Greenbelt Middle Schools, Prince George's County Public Schools, MD (French, German, Japanese, Latin, Russian, Spanish, Swahili also offered)			

Geographical Distribution of Programs

Program Qualities

Many qualities and characteristics have contributed to the success of these programs, but at least four merit special attention. One is flexibility. Unanticipated events have often forced programs to change their well-developed plans. For example, when a shift in the state's priorities and mandates left the school district in Chapel Hill, North Carolina, without the anticipated level of support from the state, program leaders succeeded in developing such strong community support for the FLES program that the local district assumed responsibility for almost all of the necessary funding.

Another key to success is teamwork. Foreign language professionals in these programs work closely with district superintendents, members of the board of education, school principals, regular classroom teachers, parents, and others in the community. Many have formed fruitful partnerships with nearby universities, with benefits ranging from professional development opportunities and shared technical expertise to long-range articulation plans and teacher recruitment possibilities.

A third characteristic evident in all seven of the model programs is leadership. One or two individuals with a vision of foreign language teaching and learning lead(s) each of these. They inspire others and organize the people and resources necessary to build an effective program. These individuals, who are described in the following chapters, have been key to the success of their programs.

Finally, staff in these programs share a deep commitment to their programs and to the goal of providing foreign language education for young learners. Teachers and program leaders spend many hours communicating with colleagues and building the relationships that contribute to high-quality language programs. They write grant proposals and engage in other fund-raising and advocacy activities to ensure the continuation of their programs. They develop and adapt curricula that are suitable for young language learners. And they devise ingenious means of motivating and educating their students.

The chapters that follow provide concrete examples of these program qualities at work. The founders and staff of these programs want to share what they learned while developing and implementing their programs, so that others can benefit from their experience. It is hoped that other schools will adopt and adapt the ideas provided here to develop or enhance foreign language programs for young learners throughout the United States.

Overview of This Book

Each of the model programs is described in a separate chapter of this book. Some chapters include the story of how the program was developed; others emphasize specific program strengths, such as content-enriched curriculum or articulation. Each chapter includes a description of these aspects of the program:

- general characteristics of the community and the program
- program goals and philosophy
- illustrative classroom activities and samples or descriptions of curriculum outlines
- people behind the program—roles, responsibilities, and perspectives of program administrators, teachers, parents, and students
- assessment practices—how student progress is assessed and how the programs themselves are evaluated
- ongoing challenges
- keys to success

Many chapters also describe specific ways that programs incorporate the five Cs of the national standards (communication, cultures, connections, comparisons, and communities) into their teaching and provide examples of student work, suggestions for parents, and other items of interest.

It is important to note that language learning activities described in classroom vignettes in each chapter are not just a collection of frivolous fun and games. These lessons were frequently special events or the culminating activity of a thematic unit. One characteristic of all seven programs is that lesson activities are carefully sequenced, and each lesson is based on carefully developed curricular guidelines, building on previously learned material and helping to develop skills for subsequent learning. As Kathleen Riordan, Foreign Language Director of Springfield (MA) Public Schools, says, "The activities have to be more than busy work or fun; they must have a purpose."

Facts about the programs and quotes from teachers, principals, other school staff, parents, and students are based on interviews and other information-gathering activities carried out during site visits to each program in 1998. In most instances, students' real names have not been used.

A concluding chapter summarizes lessons learned by the programs in 10 areas:

- Implementing national standards
- Student assessment
- Teaching methods
- Articulation
- Funding
- Program evaluation
- Use of technology
- Advocacy
- Staff development
- Incorporating content from other subjects into language curricula

In this concluding chapter, readers can quickly identify effective strategies or promising directions in a specific area of program design, implementation, or evaluation.

Appendices provide background information on the model schools project, selected materials from two programs (scanned exactly as received from the programs), a table summarizing the features of the seven programs, and contact information for each of the programs.

Bay Point Elementary School

Pinellas County Public Schools, St. Petersburg, Florida

Twenty-five enthusiastic third graders file into the classroom clutching imitation passports, plane tickets, and small suitcases, eager to board a plane to Mexico. The smiling teacher at the classroom door chats with them in Spanish, asking about their destinations and occupations as she checks passports and collects tickets. The students scramble to find their assigned seats in the airplane outlined in masking tape on the classroom floor, and soon the teacher pantomimes closing the aircraft door. She welcomes her passengers to this flight, and after announcing the rules about smoking and fastening seat belts, she pushes the PLAY button of the cassette player, which then roars with sounds of a plane taking off.

Once *piloto automático* kicks in, the teacher turns on an educational video about Mexican life for the students to watch as she makes her way down the aisle with a cart of snacks—tostitos, salsa, and soda. After the movie, students review information about Mexico, such as the capital city, the colors of the flag, names of the indigenous groups who live in the south, and traditional dances. Soon, more taped sound effects indicate that the plane has landed.

Now on Mexican soil, the teacher leads the students in a rendition of "La Bamba," encouraging them to follow the lyrics on a colorful poster. Then a small group of the third graders put on sombreros and dance with the teacher, entertaining the other young visitors to Mexico. Soon, everyone reboards the plane for the return flight.

2.01 ▪

"La Bamba"
Para bailar la bamba . . . Para bailar la bamba
se necesita una poca de gracia,
una poca de gracia y otra cosita.

CORO:
Ay arriba . . . arriba.
Ay arriba y arriba, arriba iré,
Yo no soy marinero.
Yo no soy marinero, soy capitán.
Soy capitán, soy capitán
BAMBA BAMBA . . . BAMBA BAMBA.

En mi casa me dicen . . . En mi casa me dicen
el inocente por que tengo chamacas.
Por que tengo chamacas de quince y veinte,
CORO

Para subir al cielo, para subir al cielo
se necesita una escalera larga.
Una escalera larga y otra chiquita
CORO

La Bamba (traditional Mexican song)

Now students answer questions about Mexico as they are prompted to look out the windows and identify the Sierra Madre Oriental Mountains, the Gulf of Mexico, and other geographical features. After landing in the United States, everyone applauds. In closing, students talk about their trip to Mexico, describing what they saw and did. Students are given a sticker to place in their passports, indicating that they have visited Mexico. In addition to completing a lesson rich in vocabulary and culture, students have learned a bit about traveling to a Spanish-speaking country.

Program Overview

This lesson is an example of the content-enriched Spanish FLES (Foreign Language in Elementary School) program at Bay Point Elementary School, a magnet school for math, science, technology, and foreign language in St. Petersburg, Florida. Pinellas County is an urban school district with 106,687 students (1997-1998); 33% of the students qualify for free or reduced-price lunch. Of Bay Point's 799 students, 355 are from the school attendance zone; the remaining 444 were selected by lottery from throughout the school district. In 1997-98, 62% of the students at Bay Point were Caucasian, 33% African American, 2% Hispanic American, and 2% Asian American.

All Bay Point students (Grades K–5) have 20 to 30 minutes of Spanish instruction each day. The language lessons are carefully linked to content instruction in other subjects, with the language taught in a meaningful context based on themes relevant to the children's interests and needs. Teachers use visuals, realia, songs, and drama that help children with different learning styles to learn in an enjoyable, non-threatening environment.

Program Philosophy and Goals

The Bay Point program was founded on four key beliefs:
* Young children will readily accept foreign language study and will develop increased cognitive skills as a result of learning a new language. Early foreign language instruction supports academic achievement in general and leads to foreign language proficiency.
* Starting foreign language instruction at a young age is important to achieving proficiency: The longer the students study the language, the more proficient they will become.

- For effective early foreign language learning, there should be daily instruction conducted entirely in the target language.
- Children should be encouraged and supported in learning at their own rate.

The primary purposes of the program are to expose elementary students to another language and culture and to reinforce the students' own language and culture. Bay Point program staff hope that language study will not only improve the communicative abilities of the students but also encourage love for and further study of the language.

These are the specific goals of the program:
- To support academic content area instruction (math, science, technology, language arts, social studies, art, and music)
- To develop increased cognitive skills
- To enhance reading development in both English and Spanish
- To promote global awareness and cross-cultural understanding
- To develop increased functional proficiency in all aspects of the language with each year of study
- To meet district, state, and national foreign language standards of communication, culture, connections, communities, and comparisons
- To support the district plan, which includes high student achievement, partnerships, a high-performing work force, a safe learning environment, and an integrated management system

(Pinellas County Schools, 1998, p. iii)

Spanish was selected as the language of study because of the large Hispanic community in Florida, and because, after English, Spanish is the most widely used language in the local area. Further, district schools were surveyed to identify teachers who were either bilingual or proficient in another language and could be trained in elementary foreign language teaching. Results showed that Spanish was clearly the language for which there were the most potentially qualified teachers.

In the Classroom
Schedules

Students in kindergarten through second grade have 20 minutes of Spanish instruction each day; third and fourth graders have 25 minutes; fifth graders have a half hour. Each of the four foreign language (FLES) team members at Bay Point teaches eight class periods a day, usually traveling from one classroom to another with a materials cart. The teachers have an instructional planning period and a short break for lunch, which they usually spend exchanging information about the morning classes and planning for the afternoon. Much of their materials preparation is done together after the school day.

The FLES team also meets once a month with regular classroom teachers to plan for instruction that integrates foreign language study with the regular curriculum. In addition, they use articulation forms on which regular classroom teachers indicate the content they are working on and would like to have reinforced in the foreign language class.

Curriculum

The Spanish curriculum for each grade includes a performance objective, a specific cultural emphasis, curriculum integration, and content/linguistic focus (with suggested vocabulary and activities), as well as suggested resources. Foreign language instruction is linked to all content area subjects taught in the regular curriculum. For example, when numbers are covered in the first grade curriculum, the students learn numbers in Spanish as well. Fifth graders studying ants and spiders in science learn to talk about them in Spanish, too. History, geography, and culture are also taught in Spanish class, although with less formal linkages to the regular classroom curriculum. Throughout the school year, Spanish and the other subjects share themes, such as spring, the circus, discoveries, celebrations, new worlds, moving around, "my house," and the state of Florida.

The Spanish curriculum is based on statements of specific expectations for foreign language learners at each grade level for each of the five Cs of the national foreign language standards (National Standards in Foreign Language Education Project, 1996). For example, it is expected that fourth-grade students will be able to do the following in the area of comparisons:

- Recognize that languages use different patterns to communicate and apply this knowledge to their own language
- Identify cognates related to parts of the house and household items
- Compare and contrast patterns of behavior of the target and native cultures related to family living
- Compare and contrast objects from the target culture, such as kitchen utensils

(Pinellas County Public Schools, n.d.)

2.02 ■

The Five Cs in the Bay Point Program

Communication *in languages other than English.* During language lessons all communication is in Spanish. Aside from regular class activities, there are Spanish-speaking visitors, e-mail correspondence with native-Spanish-speaking peers, and daily school announcements in Spanish by fifth graders. Teachers continue to communicate in Spanish with a number of students via e-mail throughout the summer.

Connections *with other disciplines and acquisition of information.* At Bay Point, the language class content is closely linked with the other magnet school focus areas: math, science, and technology. Shared themes, such as spring, discoveries, and the state of Florida, bring these subjects together throughout the school year.

Comparisons *that develop insight into the nature of language and culture.* The curriculum and lesson activities encourage comparison of Spanish and English languages and cultures. Comparisons are made between the United States and Spanish-speaking countries in such areas as food, dance, clothing, traditions, and geography. Activities such as fantasy trips reflect a different in-depth cultural focus for students each year, as they learn about Mexico, Spain, South America, Central America, and Puerto Rico. There is an increased focus on noting similarities and differences among the cultures throughout the program.

Knowledge and understanding of other **cultures**. Students see films about each of the Spanish-speaking countries as they study them. In addition, cultural content is woven into other lessons through songs, drama, and stories. Teachers have access to nearly 400 Spanish films from the district resource library.

Participation in multilingual **communities** *at home and around the world*. Students practice their language with Spanish-speaking community members, and native Spanish speakers volunteer their time to visit the schools and talk with the students. Some Bay Point teachers outside the FLES program are also native speakers of Spanish, and FLES students have opportunities to interact with them in Spanish. Students learn about people and communities around the world through e-mail exchanges, particularly with e-mail buddies in classes in Panama, with whom they also exchange pictures, t-shirts, and biographies.

The Five Cs

Classroom Environment

Although the Spanish teachers have to transport their teaching materials from room to room on carts, many of the regular teachers help out by incorporating language-related decorations in the classrooms. The student work displayed on classroom walls is in both Spanish and English. There are signs, posters, and other decorations with numbers, months, holidays, and rooms of the house, all identified in Spanish. In addition, most regular classrooms have five computer stations, a television and VCR, bookshelves of textbooks, student art work displays, print-rich bulletin boards, and other grade-level appropriate materials.

The FLES teachers may not have individual classrooms, but they do have Café Olé. Used for technology-related classes, theatrical presentations and rehearsals, and Spanish Club meetings, Café Olé is a stand-alone, realia-rich classroom that also serves as the Spanish teachers' office and materials room. A quick glance around Café Olé reveals a Spanish flag, globes, computer stations, a television and VCR, and a menagerie of stuffed animals corresponding to those covered in the regular curriculum. Near the teachers' desks are several long racks of coat hangers draped with hundreds of song and lesson charts. Beneath the hanging materials are huge boxes of labeled envelopes filled with instructional materials from past lessons. There are Spanish posters and signs on the walls and child-size furniture for a bathroom, bedroom, and kitchen, all labeled in Spanish. Each Spanish teacher has the Café Olé classroom one day a week for special classes, such as the fantasy trip to Mexico, that combine technology with foreign language instruction.

Special Programs and Events

Special program activities and events provide an opportunity to highlight student accomplishments in the program in a way that parents, other teachers, administrators, and the community can understand and enjoy. These events include talent nights, an economics fair, fiestas, and the yearly Magnet School Fair at the local mall, where principals promote their programs and students perform. There is also a yearly spring concert, a hilarious Halloween program based on the Addams Family theme, and Spanish Club presentations, such as a Rosie O'Donnell show in Spanish featuring performances from Bay Point students playing Rosie, the Spice Girls, and Leonardo DiCaprio.

Club Olé (Spanish Club)

Club Olé is a voluntary after-school Spanish language club where students and teachers continue to use the foreign language as they work on special foreign language activities, practice and perform talent shows and presentations, and take field trips. Club Olé activities have included performing for Governor Jeb Bush at their school, performing at the school fair, and taking a field trip to a Mexican restaurant with money raised from lollipop sales. Due to space constraints and logistical difficulties, membership is limited to 40–50 children, distributed over all grades, with a particular emphasis on fifth grade. Because so many children want to join, there is a selection process twice a year so that a larger number of students will have a chance to participate each year. Membership is by lottery, but preference is given to children who are willing to perform, sing, and show off.

Teaching Methods and Approaches

Spanish instruction is proficiency oriented, meaning there is a greater focus on meaningful and purposeful communication than on grammatical mastery. The program content and design show the strong influence of Curtain and Pesola's book, *Languages and Children: Making the Match: Foreign Language Instruction for an Early Start (Grades K–8)* (1994). In fact, Helena Curtain conducted early staff development activities for the foreign language teachers and administrators at Bay Point. In line with Krashen's Natural Approach (Krashen & Terrell, 1983), teachers make sure to provide opportunities for students to hear and speak the language just at or slightly above their current level of comprehension in a communicative, meaningful, and engaging context. Students are encouraged first to understand the language and show their comprehension by responding to simple questions, then to produce language when they are ready. Classes focus on listening and speaking, and on thematic learning that reinforces the regular elementary curriculum while incorporating information about Spanish-speaking cultures.

Teachers plan activities to appeal to all of the senses: sight, hearing, touch, taste, and smell. Some lessons use Total Physical Response activities, which have the children pointing, pantomiming, or moving about the room. During a lesson on sea animals, for example, the students see and touch bright-colored stuffed sea animals, and when they hear the Spanish word for the movements the animals make, they wiggle, slither, and dive.

2.03 ■

Grade level: First
Unit: Science—"Bajo el mar"
Lesson: Identification of sea animal
Use of verbs that describe actions of sea animals

National Standard (Student Expectation):
Students engage in conversations, provide and obtain information, express feelings and emotions, and exchange opinions.

Specific Lesson Outcome:
Students will be able to provide information about the animals drawn in the class books.

Lesson Plan

Warm-up: "Sí, sí, sí" song
Calendar/weather
Assessment

Review: 1) "Bajo el mar" song
2) "Los pajaritos" poem
—Class adds verses to poem, coming up with verbs that describe actions of animals in the new verses.

Core: Read class books
—Students attempt to identify the animal drawn in the book, then name an action that goes with the particular animal.

Evaluation: Students naming animals and actions in core lesson.

Closing: "Adiós mis estudiantes" song

Spanish is used exclusively by teachers during foreign language class periods, and students are expected to use only Spanish as well. To encourage this, the teacher awards the class a *Todo en Español* green slip at the end of a lesson if everyone has used only Spanish. After earning enough *Todo en Español* slips, the class is rewarded with a special technology- or theater-related foreign language class in the Café Olé classroom.

Particularly in the lower grades, academic reading, writing, and grammar are kept to a minimum in Spanish class. There are textbooks and some handouts that include the written language, but Spanish reading skills are learned implicitly rather than through specific reading activities. Reading is emphasized more in the upper grades. For example, Spanish language science texts were recently purchased to supplement the fifth grade science curriculum. Similarly, although the teacher does not teach a lesson on adverbial and verb endings, the students learn them as they sing or recite rhymes and songs, or as they see the endings spelled correctly on a song or story chart.

Language Learning Activities

Taking a fantasy plane trip to another country with ticket, passport, and a small suitcase is one of the more elaborate activities. Others are creative but less time-consuming to prepare. To review colors, the teacher puts big colored circles on the floor and has students step or jump into each color that she calls out. To review numbers, students try to guess the number of fingers the teacher has behind her back. Alternatively, they try to predict the number that will be on a piece of paper that appears in a magic box after the teacher's "abracadabra" incantation and tap with a wand. To review sea animals, students play a memory game, matching pairs of sea animals on a board. These review activities enable students to participate confidently as the lessons proceed to more substantive content-enriched concepts, such as classification of animals or making numerical comparisons.

One innovative way that students in the foreign language program use technology is to produce a video news program in Spanish that airs during the school's morning announcements. The adjacent Bay Point Magnet Middle School has a studio where staff have trained fifth graders, who act as announcers for weather segments, the date, current events, school news, and information about Café Olé.

Videotape, Audiotape, and Computer Software
Video

La Familia Contenta is a Spanish video instructional program developed by the district foreign language teachers. It airs fairly regularly on the district television station, connecting parents and the community to the foreign language learning of the students. Children come to school excited, saying "I saw you on TV last night!" to their foreign language teachers.

The three videotapes feature Bay Point and Perkins Elementary foreign language teachers in a dramatic presentation filmed by students with technical help from county media services. The topics of the videos include: Family, Occupation/Store, Zoo, and Grocery Store. In the classroom, the videos are first presented in their entirety and then broken down into smaller segments. Teachers ask comprehension questions, and students complete cloze exercises. The TV screen is covered while the audio is played and students pantomime appropriate actions. Finally, children are encouraged to select parts and role play them, using their own vocabulary. As followup, children write a script and present it in context.

Audio

The teachers have taken traditional melodies from Spanish-speaking cultures and added their own lyrics, which young language learners can understand and enjoy. They have recorded the songs, and they use the cassette tapes and lyric books in classes to supplement authentic songs and poems. (Ordering information for videotapes and song books is available at http://www.geocities.com/Athens/Acropolis/8714.)

Software

The Bay Point FLES program uses a number of commercial materials, such as The Wiggle Works software program and the Primary All in One Language Fun! (Playing with Language Series, Syracuse Language Systems Program). Other materials include the Muzzy Spanish video course. Older grades use Laureate Learning Systems 1st Verbs, *Mi Pueblo: Actividades lingüísticas de la vida diaria.* The Grandma and Me Series by Brøderbund's Living Books and Sitting on the Farm series by Learn-Sanctuary Woods are also used.

Assessing Student Achievement
The Home Assessment System

Developed on the premise that individual children acquire language in different ways and at different rates, the Home Assessment System provides ongoing assessment of student progress. In addition, this system makes the regular classroom teachers and parents active partners in the students' foreign language learning. A letter is sent to parents explaining the purpose of the system and asking for their participation. (See 2.04.)

Attached to the parent letter is a sheet of performance activity cards (see 2.05). Activities are at 10 different language levels, with 10 performance activities to complete at each level. When the children accomplish an activity (e.g., "I can name three farm animals"), the parents cut the card from the sheet, sign and date it, and have their children return it to the school. The children then file the cards on a pocket chart in the regular classroom. As the cards are filed, the regular classroom teacher will practice or review the activity on that card with the student who has accomplished it. The foreign language teachers may also quiz a few students at the beginning of the Spanish lesson to make sure that they can complete the activity easily and accurately.

Children take pride in accumulating the cards, which eventually form a portfolio that can be passed on to middle school and high school foreign language teachers, documenting what the students have

2.04 ■

Dear Parents,

¡Hola! We are pleased to inform you that your child's teacher has volunteered to participate in the home assessment program for Spanish. The purpose of the program is to provide children with the opportunity to practice Spanish at home, thereby assisting you to assess your child's progress in Spanish, and to involve the classroom teacher in the practice of basic Spanish skills throughout the school day. Since the Spanish lesson is only between 20–30 minutes daily, this additional home and classroom practice is essential in order for children to acquire maximum proficiency.

Attached you will find the first sheet of "performance activity cards." Please read each performance activity and keep the sheet for future reference. As you feel your child has accomplished and successfully shared each activity with you, please cut the appropriate card from the sheet, fill in the required information, and return it to school with your child. He/she will be instructed to file the card behind his name in a pocket chart located in his classroom. Children will collect as many cards as possible in this manner. Once filed in the pocket chart, cards will be used by the classroom teacher for classroom practice. The accumulation of cards should become a source of pride for your child, much like a portfolio.

Children should be under no pressure to complete skills until they are ready, and parents should not be overly concerned with accuracy, since all skills are practiced and monitored extensively in the Spanish classroom. Because children new to Bay Point may be in the same class with children who have studied Spanish for several years (with the exception of kindergarten), there are no deadlines for completion of performance activity sheets.

We hope that, with the information we are able to offer you via this format, your child might be able to share with you some of what he/she is learning. Your encouragement should help your child to achieve even greater future success. Thank you for your help and HAPPY SHARING!

Pinellas County (FL) FLES Team, 1997

Parent Letter (Home Assessment)

2.05 ■

I can say what I ate for breakfast. Name: .... Date: .... Parent's Signature:	**I can name five foods that are served in our school cafeteria.** Name: .... Date: .... Parent's Signature: ....
I can describe (order) a well-balanced dinner. Name: .... Date: .... Parent's Signature:	**I can name 5 modes of transportation.** Name: .... Date: .... Parent's Signature: ....
I can name the planets in Spanish. Name: .... Date: .... Parent's Signature:	**I can name the Spanish speaking countries of North and Central America.** Name: .... Date: .... Parent's Signature: ....
I can name the four seasons in Spanish. Name: .... Date: .... Parent's Signature:	**I can say four different rooms of the house in Spanish.** Name: .... Date: .... Parent's Signature: ....
I can say a sentence about what my mom or dad does for a living. Name: .... Date: .... Parent's Signature:	**I can say four objects in the kitchen in Spanish.** Name: .... Date: .... Parent's Signature: ....
I can desribe the contents of my backpack. Name: .... Date: .... Parent's Signature:	**I can name all the Spanish speaking countries in the continent of South America.** Name: .... Date: .... Parent's Signature: ....
I can describe a spring day with 4 phrases. Name: .... Date: .... Parent's Signature:	**I can say four objects in the living room in Spanish.** Name: .... Date: .... Parent's Signature: ....

Sample Assessment Cards

accomplished. By working through the performance activity cards, new students are able to catch up with their peers at their own pace. Children and their parents can use the home assessment system as a tool for informal review of recent material or even from one year to the next. Teachers and administrators use it as one element of program evaluation, because it provides a record of specific student achievements that reflect program objectives.

Home Assessment Calendar

For younger children (Grades K–2), a monthly calendar is sent home to parents listing things the children should be able to do. Parents can review these activities with their children, which keeps them aware of what their children are learning and involves them in the learning process. The parents send the homework calendars back to school at the end of month.

Grade level performance objectives are indicated in the Home Assessment System, but students are not expected to meet these objectives according to a rigid timetable. For example, a student may complete a number of the higher level objectives before attempting some of the ones listed for a lower grade level. Students are not required to show their class results to a parent unless the parent requests it. The information remains in the student's portfolio.

Other Assessment

To complement the Home Assessment System, teachers use outcome rubrics to document student performance during various group and paired activities. Five different types of outcome rubrics are used:

- Paired activity (students negotiate meaning in the target language to complete a paired activity)
- Performance (students demonstrate comprehension of language through performance of a song, mime, dialogue, or drama piece)
- Fantasy trip (students demonstrate comprehension and use of language through participation in a fantasy trip)

- Content (students demonstrate a content-area skill in the target language)
- Publishing (students develop or create a product using the target language)

Each of the rubrics has six or seven objectives on which the teacher rates student performance as *exemplary, acceptable,* or *not yet.* The teacher completes the rubrics after activities such as a fantasy trip. The rubrics are used primarily for program evaluation rather than for individual evaluation. Rubrics help teachers decide if they need to change instructional activities for specific lessons.

In addition, a Pinellas County FLES Program Exit Rubric for fifth grade lists 50 separate performance outcomes for students. There is a place for the student, peer, and teacher to indicate what the student can do in Spanish. (See Appendix 2 for examples of these rubrics.)

The People Behind the Program
The Foreign Language Teachers

In Pinellas County Schools, elementary foreign language teachers are required to be either elementary school certified native speakers or to be certified in the target language and have native or near-native proficiency. Local universities play an important role in providing teacher training programs near the district schools. Teachers in the program have been recruited from the University of South Florida, which has a highly regarded elementary foreign language teacher training program. There has been almost no teacher turnover in the program. Two of the teachers are native speakers of Spanish from Cuba and Puerto Rico; the other two are native English speakers with native-like proficiency in Spanish.

At Bay Point Elementary, the four foreign language teachers are responsible for all grades, kindergarten through fifth. In addition to providing instruction, the teachers have responsibilities in four other areas. First, they work with the other classroom teachers to integrate foreign language instruction with the rest of the curriculum. They provide staff development sessions for the regular teachers to keep them involved and informed, encouraging their collaboration. Second, they are the primary link to parents, keeping them informed and involved in their children's language learning. Third, they coordinate with the principal and the magnet program coordinator regarding such issues as budget matters, record keeping, and articulation with upper level schools. Finally, the foreign language team works with the district foreign language supervisor to develop district-wide curricula, design assessments, and provide input on state foreign language standards and standards-based assessments.

The Regular Classroom Teachers

Because the regular classroom teachers remain in the classroom during the Spanish lessons, they see firsthand how the content and themes they are teaching are reinforced through the foreign language. Acknowledging the benefits of this linkage, teachers are generally very appreciative and supportive of the foreign language program, even willing to advocate for it. "Foreign language definitely adds to—and never subtracts from—the regular classroom instruction," says one teacher. According to the classroom teachers, foreign language is so popular with the children that "they are extremely disappointed if anything keeps them from their Spanish class."

The regular classroom teachers and foreign language teachers communicate both informally and formally about how to reinforce content in the Spanish lessons. The teachers chat about their classes before or after the foreign language lesson, during lunch, or while passing in the halls. The more formal system involves a communication form called "Let's articulate," which the classroom teachers fill out regularly. Teachers indicate here what the focus of instruction will be in the regular classroom during specific months, list content areas to be covered, and make helpful suggestions or comments for the Spanish teacher.

2.06 ■

> ## Let's articulate . . . . . .
>
> Name . . . .
>
> Grade Level . . . .
>
> Much of my instruction will deal with the following theme(s): . . . .
>
> . . . . during the month(s) of:
> (if applicable)
>
> **August September October November December January February March April May**
>
> I will be working with the following content during ths time period:
>
> Math . . . . Science . . . .
> Social studies . . . . Language arts . . . . Other . . . .
>
> I have the following suggestion for the FLES teacher: . . . .
> Pinellas County FLES Team/1996

■
Let's articulate…

Classroom teachers also try to build on foreign language instruction by linking it to regular instruction after the Spanish lesson ends. For example, one teacher uses Spanish words as bonus words for spelling bees and reviews numbers in Spanish. The classroom teachers also participate in the Home Assessment System and quiz their students on the vocabulary they have been studying in Spanish class.

The Parents

The program reaches out to parents through a welcome letter (see Appendix 2) and newsletter articles. For example, one article addresses concerns that parents might have about the language learning process and what to expect from their children's classes. Another explains how parents can participate in their child's learning through the Home Assessment System. Another praises students for their participation in developing a Spanish video program and for using Spanish while serving a meal to guests at a school-wide event.

Parents help their children practice their Spanish at home by using phrases they have picked up (often from the children themselves) to ask their children questions, such as "Have you cleaned your room?" and "What's for dinner?" They also quiz them on the home assessment cards that the children bring home. Parents encourage language learning and practice at home in other ways, as well. Among the resources they may have at home for their children are Disney sing-along tapes and videos in Spanish, small books purchased at the school book fair, computer programs, a Spanish/English dictionary, and the music tapes and books produced by the Bay Point program. Children may watch the Spanish channel at home and talk with siblings who have studied Spanish also.

Parents who were interviewed say that their children use Spanish for more than just reviewing their lessons. They hear them around the house singing Spanish songs and repeating poems that they have learned in class. They also use Spanish on vacation and in the community with native Spanish speakers. At school, the children speak Spanish with friends, classmates, teachers, and on teams. When visitors ask why the children believe foreign language learning is important, they say, "It's cool to know another language."

The majority of the parents are very involved at the school, particularly in special events. One parent has produced a foreign language newsletter, and many sit in on Club Olé meetings and rehearsals. They have also helped with fundraising for a lunch-time field trip to a Mexican restaurant.

Parents support and advocate for the program because they are impressed with how communicative and excited their children have become about foreign language learning. Parents call the program "beyond excellent" and "one of the strongest programs that we have here." Several years ago the district announced plans to use technology to present language instruction instead of hiring needed personnel. Parents responded by inviting the superintendent to the school to discuss their opposition to the proposal. The superintendent went back to the district with their comments, and the additional teachers were hired for the program.

The District Foreign Language Supervisor

Since the mid-1980s, Carmine Zinn, the district foreign language supervisor, has had a vision for an elementary foreign language program and a commitment to advocating for it and taking the necessary steps to put it in place. With extensive foreign language teaching experience in Grades K–12 and strong professional involvement in the foreign language field at the local, state, and national levels, Zinn was aware of elementary foreign language programs around the country, and she was eager to see the children in the Pinellas County schools benefit from such a program.

She began by educating the district superintendent, deputy superintendent, and school board about the advantages of early foreign language instruction for children. She received their backing, as well as the cooperation and support of parents and regular classroom teachers. She wrote a proposal in 1986 to apply for a State Elementary Foreign Language grant, which provided the initial program funding beginning in 1987. Severe budget cuts in 1991 led to the closing of the program during the 1992-93 school year, but the pilot program laid the foundation for the current program, which began in 1993 with funding from the district's Magnet Schools Assistance Program.

During the pilot program, Zinn purchased most of the core program materials, coordinated staff development, and oversaw curriculum coordination and program planning. Time for curriculum development and planning was crucial to building a strong foundation for the program. Initially, one day a week was available for instructional planning and curriculum writing because the foreign language teachers had fewer classes to teach and more time for such activities. As one grade level was added each year of the program, the teachers spent more time in the classroom and had less time available for collaborative planning.

At present, however, most of the curriculum has already been developed and less planning time is needed. Now, one of Carmine Zinn's most important roles is as a program resource and contact person. As they plan their lessons, teachers call on her with questions, problems, or requests for advice. The office of the foreign language supervisor also funds development of new assessment tools, staff development activities, and updating of the curriculum to incorporate the national standards for foreign language learning and the Florida foreign language standards (State of Florida, 1996). "I would especially like to see more staff development activities that focus on using technology [in foreign language instruction]," Zinn says.

The School Principal, the Magnet Coordinator, and the School Board

As the principal of Bay Point Elementary School, Gaye Lively is responsible for promoting the foreign language program in the community, for developing community organization partnerships, for strengthening the articulation between foreign language and regular classroom teachers, and for ensuring that the school's improvement plan is implemented.

With funds provided by the district, Lively oversees the school budget, which involves dividing funds among the different magnet focus areas. The foreign language program portion of the budget includes items such as instructional materials, classroom resources, additional workbooks, technology, software, hardware, a website, and a webmaster.

Lively also has a role in curriculum decisions and says that she is pleased with how well the FLES team has integrated the foreign language and regular curricula. She makes sure that each magnet focus area (math, science, technology, and foreign language) has curriculum training sessions each month, which are open to all school staff. The foreign language sessions focus on language acquisition, content-enriched instruction, and Spanish language lessons. "I know that the foreign language trainings are very popular," Lively says. "During the year, over 50% of the school's teachers and support services staff attended voluntarily."

The magnet coordinator, Linda Evers, oversees all four of the school's magnet area programs. In conjunction with the district foreign language supervisor, the magnet coordinator plans for articulation between the elementary and middle school foreign language programs. Evers maintains academic and demographic statistics on the students and shares budget and curriculum coordination responsibilities with the principal.

Although not involved in the daily operations of the foreign language program, the Pinellas County School Board plays an important role in its continuation. The seven board members approve and provide funding for teacher salaries and materials. They approve the budget and the staffing model. Although the board is generally supportive of the magnet program, members always have to balance it with other district needs. One school board member says, "We are especially interested in tangible results showing that foreign language enhances academic achievement in other areas."

When the district budget was cut severely in 1991, the school board decided by a single vote to discontinue the pilot program for the 1992-93 academic year, despite an excellent program evaluation, strong parent support, and community advocacy efforts at school board meetings. It was only with the securing of magnet school funding that the foreign language program was revived the following year.

Challenges

As the 1991 budget cut illustrates, Bay Point Elementary School and Pinellas County Schools are not immune to the difficulties faced by other public schools in the United States. Four problem areas that have been particularly challenging to Bay Point's foreign language program are funding, program evaluation and accountability, articulation, and changes in the student population.

Funding

One of the biggest challenges is maintaining a program that is consistent despite varying levels of funding and support. Teacher salaries are the largest cost involved in running the foreign language program. The cost for instructional materials and supplies was approximately $5,000 in 1997-98. More had to be spent in this area during the start-up phase of the program when texts, technology (computers, printers, laser disc player, TV, VCR, camcorder, and tape recorders), and other essential items had to be purchased. During the earlier pilot program, paying staff to write curriculum was another major expense.

Magnet school funds of approximately $10,000 per year are divided among science, technology, math, and foreign language, with technology usually receiving the bulk of the funds. Currently, the magnet funds are provided by the district to the school, and the school allocates funds to the various magnet programs, as needed.

Program Evaluation and Accountability

Although the elementary foreign language pilot program was evaluated twice during the 1980s, the current program has not been the subject of a formal evaluation. Teachers and students chart their growth through the district's PSDA (plan, study, do, act) formula and through the Student Achievement Model. Teachers are being trained in data collection so that they can use the information for improving instruction. They set goals and look at the results continuously as part of ongoing informal evaluation. In addition, teachers use rubrics as a means of monitoring how effective their teaching activities have been. (See earlier section on Assessing Student Achievement.) Meanwhile, the state is focusing on traditional testing in most subject areas and is rating schools according to test scores.

Articulation

Students in the Pinellas County School District have the opportunity to study foreign language from Grades K–12, but the elementary to middle school transition has been weak. With only two middle schools that offer linking foreign language programs, opportunities for continuation are limited. The students who do well in the elementary FLES program remain together in special classes during middle school, but even for them, the transition has not been ideal. In contrast to the emphasis on communication activities in elementary school Spanish instruction, middle school lessons tend to have a more formal textbook focus, emphasizing accuracy of grammar and spelling more than communication. Perhaps most important, elementary and middle school teachers have not had opportunities to collaborate to plan instruction that links to and reinforces what was learned in the elementary school program.

Recognizing this problem, the district supervisor has implemented processes to facilitate the transition from the K–5 program to the middle school. She has met with the middle school foreign language teachers to discuss what the students coming out of the K–5 program can do, looking at their test results, home assessments, and portfolios. The middle school teachers are learning how to develop a stronger bridge for these students as they plan instruction that is more communicative and that builds on what has been learned in the elementary program. Setting aside time for program planning has been important in working toward this goal.

Program staff hope that Bay Point students will continue on to the advanced foreign language programs at St. Petersburg's two magnet international baccalaureate high schools. Students must meet a foreign language proficiency requirement to be eligible for these programs, making it necessary in middle school for them to choose foreign language study over other activities like music and art. Although articulation is a challenge, efforts are underway to meet that challenge.

Changing Student Population

The Bay Point foreign language program has attracted many parents and children from outside the local neighborhood and enjoys wide community support. This kind of support may change as the school population increases and as admission is opened to increasing numbers of students from the neighborhood area. In addition, the Bay Point program has been challenged by the transient neighborhood population, which results in transfers and new students with no previous foreign language education joining the foreign language program in the higher grade levels.

2.07

Integrating New Students

During the first week and a half of classes in the school year, students new to Bay Point participate in a special program. For these 10 days, there is no foreign language instruction in the regular classrooms. Instead, all new students meet with the foreign language teachers in the Café Olé classroom for intensive, personalized instruction. They are taught language learning strategies as well as some of the core foreign language material already covered by the other students. The teachers let them know before they enter the regular classes that they are not expected to produce the language right away, and that they are not expected to have achieved the same level of proficiency as the other children. New students are also encouraged to make special use of computer programs and materials at home and at school to aid them in their language study. They are able to select areas to work on by consulting materials from the Home Assessment System. Additionally, each new student is assigned a buddy in the class who acts as a partner and model in the language learning process.

Keys to Success

By any standard, the foreign language program at Bay Point Elementary School is excellent. Several elements have contributed to its success:

- Vision and commitment from the district foreign language supervisor
- Clear articulation of program philosophy and goals
- Funding for materials
- Time for staff to develop curricula
- Committed, well-qualified staff, who are also creative and energetic
- Creative, communicative teaching activities
- Multi-faceted, self-paced assessment procedures
- Positive relationships and coordination with regular classroom teachers
- Attention to state and national standards
- Outreach to and involvement of parents and the community

Perhaps the single most important element has been teamwork. The foreign language program was designed by the foreign language supervisor and the foreign language teachers as a team. Together, they brought a high level of foreign language and elementary teaching experience and know-how to the tasks of designing curricula, identifying materials, and developing an instructional plan that reinforces the regular elementary curriculum. The teachers worked together to develop foreign language lessons that enhance content instruction at each grade level, creating a vast number of visuals, posters, charts, and other materials to support the program. Now the team has expanded to include regular classroom teachers, administrators, parents, the students, and the community. All are contributing to make this model program a success.

Springfield Public Schools

Springfield, Massachusetts

Elementary school students in Springfield, Massachusetts, have a number of reasons for finding their foreign language classes useful. Alex Fleet has already been a "ring boy" in a Spanish wedding and loves Spanish food. Jaleezah Smith is looking forward to becoming a doctor, and she wants to be able to talk to her patients. Maria Lopez would like to understand her grandmother's stories better, and Nick Stefanopoulos wants to do well in high school "and then maybe I'll get a scholarship to a good college." Jaleezah and Alex are fourth graders at Sumner Avenue School; Nick and Maria are fifth graders at Armory Street School. All four see foreign language as a key to enjoying enriching experiences and achieving their dreams. Jaleezah has been studying Spanish since preschool; the others started foreign language learning in third grade. "Learning a language is also fun, especially the songs," Jaleezah adds.

Program Overview

These students are participating in a program of content-enriched foreign language instruction that is being implemented not only at Armory Street and Sumner Avenue Elementary Schools, but in all 32 elementary schools in Springfield, Massachusetts. Every Springfield student in first through fifth grade spends 90 minutes per week in foreign language study. Language classes are scheduled for 30-minute sessions three times per week or 45-minute sessions two times per week. Apart from one school that offers only French, all elementary schools in Springfield offer Spanish. Four schools offer both French and Spanish; three offer French, Spanish, and Chinese. These elementary school language programs link to language programs in the sixth through twelfth grades.

With a population of over 150,000, Springfield is the second largest city in Massachusetts. There are over 26,000 students in the Springfield School District, approximately 80% of whom qualify for free or reduced-price lunch. Thirty-seven percent of the students are Hispanic, 31% are Caucasian, 29% are African American, and 2% are Asian American. All elementary schools are "controlled choice" schools as part of the district's integration program. In this model, each school, including the two featured here, reflects the ethnic and racial diversity of the entire district.

Program Philosophy and Goals

Simply stated, the goals of the Springfield foreign language program are for students to communicate and to connect with others who speak the target language. Foreign language instruction is aimed at facilitating "genuine interaction with others, whether they are on another continent, across town, or within the neighborhood" (Springfield Public Schools, 1996).

The program that Springfield has implemented to meet these goals is based on three principles set forth in the introduction to the district's *World Language Learning Outcomes*, printed as a working draft in 1996. The first principle is that *"all* students will develop and maintain proficiency in English and at least one other language, modern or classical" (Springfield Public Schools, 1996). All students should be able to read, write, and converse in at least one language in addition to their first language. This competence is critical, because it enables Americans to communicate with people in other cultures in the United States as well as in other countries. Foreign language education gives people the ability to "look beyond their customary borders" while providing them with a greater awareness and understanding of their own culture and language and with access to information, experiences, and resources that are closed to people who know only one language (Springfield Public Schools, 1996).

The second principle is that "*all* students can be successful language and culture learners." In order to support this learning, the study of language and culture is integrated into the total school experience. Instructors also recognize individual differences in students' rates of learning and in their learning styles. "The student is at the center of an effective foreign language classroom" (Springfield Public Schools, 1996).

The third guiding principle of Springfield's foreign language program is that "language and culture is [sic] part of the core curriculum." Foreign language connects with all of the other disciplines. "It is built on the general curriculum rather than restricted to the foreign language curriculum," explains Kathleen Riordan, Springfield's Director of Foreign Languages (Met, 1998, p. 266). Like other subjects, foreign language education must reflect local, state, and national standards and "incorporate effective strategies, assessment procedures, and technologies" (Springfield Public Schools, 1996).

In the Classroom
Curriculum
The principles and goals of the foreign language program are reflected in Springfield Public Schools' *World Language Learning Outcomes* (Springfield Public Schools, 1996), which is based on *The Massachusetts Foreign Languages Curriculum Framework* (Massachusetts Department of Education, 1999). Springfield's outcomes document sets forth learning goals for all grades and lists age-appropriate topics, content, and types of texts for Grades K–5, 6–8, and 9–12. Under the heading "Types of Text," this framework document suggests the kinds of materials to be used for the development of lit-

eracy skills in the target language. Foreign language classes in early grades should include print matter such as posters, rhymes, and short readings. Classes in upper elementary grades are to use texts such as magazines, schedules, stories, and dictionaries, and technological resources for authentic materials.

3.01

Grades K–5 Topics and Content

Topics close to the self, the home, and the school using learned words, phrases, and expressions in social, face-to-face situations.

family
friends
home and house
classroom
animals
counting
days, dates, months
alphabet
colors and shapes
weather
festivals and holidays
myths
arts
music
games
introductions, greetings, and leave-takings
health, food, parts of the body
geography vocabulary
signs and symbols
daily routines
feelings
contact with other cultures
topics from other subject areas: science, arts, math, and social studies

Grade-level outcomes are organized according to the five strands of the national standards for foreign language learning: communication, comparisons, cultures, connections, and communities (National Standards in Foreign Language in Education Project, 1996). Each strand includes an outcome statement, progress indicators, and specified outcome assessments. For example, the outcome stated for the Communities strand for the end of Grades 3–5 is that "All students will continue to use a language in addition to their first language to participate in local and global communities." The progress indicators are that students will use the new language to prepare informative posters for the local library about regions where the target language is used; identify words from the target language used in such fields as medicine, law, and science; and identify careers where knowing more than one language is useful.

These outcomes are cumulative, so students by the end of Grades 3–5 are also expected to be able to do the activities described in the K–2 outcome statements and indicators. In this instance, the K–2 progress indicators are that students will use the language to "interact with native users of the target language inside and outside the classroom" and "participate in school/community activities." (See Appendix 3 for sample K–2 Learning Outcomes for World Languages.)

The outcome assessments specified for the Communities strand at the Grade 3–5 level include student learning logs, a teacher observation checklist, and role plays. (The full set of outcomes is available from Springfield Public Schools.)

In Springfield's 1998 *World Language Learning Outcomes* (Springfield Public Schools, 1998), topics or themes are divided by grade level, K–5. Detailed curriculum information for each theme is included under the headings of Content Areas, Outcomes, Vocabulary/Structure, Culture, Instructional Activities (including recommended textbooks and other materials), and Assessment Activities. (See Appendix 3 for a sample curriculum page for the fourth grade numbers theme: "Geometry, Measurement, and Working with Data.")

This impressively detailed curriculum is largely the result of a major initiative led by the Superintendent of Schools and the Director of Foreign Languages. In the early 1990s, Massachusetts passed an Education Reform Act, which included foreign languages as part of the core curriculum for all grades. In 1995, Springfield convened a summer workshop at which foreign language specialists and elementary teachers built on the state program to develop the district's own content-enriched curriculum and learning outcomes. They are "continuing this ongoing curriculum development work as the program evolves" (Riordan, 1998, p. 264). The fifth grade curriculum was completed in 1998.

3.02 ■ _____

The Massachusetts Foreign Languages Curriculum Framework

The Massachusetts Foreign Language Curriculum Framework has been the major source for Springfield's program design (Massachusetts Department of Education, 1999). The third edition of the framework is an 85-page booklet describing the principles, strands, and standards for foreign language programs in Massachusetts public schools. After a four-page description of the guiding principles underlying the framework, a table displays a four-stage model of language proficiency. Each stage includes descriptions of what students can be expected to do at that proficiency level. Stage 2, for instance, includes this description for modern language learners: "As they enter Stage 2, students begin to create new combinations of the language they have learned in Stage 1. Messages are understandable but some patterns of error may interfere with full comprehension" (p. 9). A note at the bottom of the page cautions that students do not progress through the stages in a smooth linear way but may move back and forth, "at one moment showing confidence and accuracy, at another moment losing both" (p. 9).

The foreign language curriculum framework is presented in five sections organized by the five content strands: Communication, Cultures, Comparisons, Connections, and Communities. In addition, eight learning standards specify what students should know or be able to do within each strand. In the Comparisons strand, for example, one learning standard states, "Students will demonstrate an understanding of the nature of language through comparison of the language studied and their own. In classical language study, discussion and writing will be in English." Much of the rest of the booklet describes in detail the expected learning outcomes at different grade and proficiency levels for the standards for each strand. Appendices include sample activities, assessment procedures, and a helpful re-casting of the framework, organized by stages rather than by strand. In addition to a well-organized bibliography, there are two particularly useful technology-related appendices. One describes a variety of uses of technology for the language teacher and learner; the second outlines "technology literacy comptetencies" as they relate to foreign language study.

                                                     ■

The Massachusetts Foreign Languages Curriculum Framework

Spanish at Sumner Avenue School

At Sumner Avenue School, William Tarnowski is responsible for all foreign language instruction, which is in Spanish. His printed schedule is a patchwork of 20- and 40-minute blocks. Typical of other foreign language teachers in Springfield elementary schools, Tarnowski is the only foreign language teacher at his school.

The 22 third graders look up at teacher Tarnowski when he enters the classroom. There is a quick exchange of *buenos días* and other expressions of greeting, and the Spanish class begins. After a few introductory remarks, Tarnowski quizzes the students about the continents and oceans. Referring to charts and pictures around the room, he asks about color, weather, and compass directions to check that students recall previous material. Raising and waving their hands, many of the children seem prepared and eager to answer, and most of their answers are completely in Spanish. Soon the group launches

3.03

El Mundo

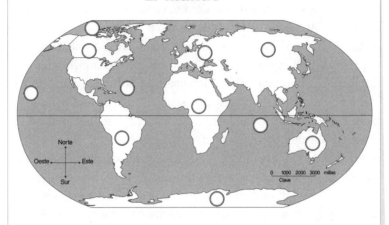

"Los Siete Continentes" Song
by Bill Tarnowski

Hay siete continentes en el mundo,
Pero yo vivo en Norteamérica.
Al sur está Sudamérica.
Al este está Europa
Y al sur de Europa está Africa.

Asia es el más grande.
Australia es el más chiquito.
Antártica es el más frío,
donde solo viven los pingüinos.

En las Amazonas hace calor.
En los polos hace frío.
Si en California hay un temblor,
No quiero estar allí! NO!!

Pero yo vivo en Norteamérica,
Estados Unidos de América.
Yo vivo en Norteamérica.

into a spirited rendition of an original teacher-composed song, *"Los Siete Continentes,"* a treatment of the geographical topic of the day. Tarnowski taps out the beat as the children gesture and sing the lyrics printed on a poster.

Next, the students place velcro labels of continents and oceans on a world map. *"¿Hay un error?"* the teacher wonders aloud, and the children scramble to put the world back in order. In a follow-up assessment activity, the children listen to statements about continents, weather, and animals and indicate their approval with *"bien"* and a thumbs up or disapproval with a *"mal"* and thumbs down. The children then move to the front of the room to add pictures and animal labels to the map. As they position the animals around the world, Tarnowski asks questions in Spanish, such as, "What kind of water do whales like?" At one point, the students stand and use their arms as compass needles to respond as the teacher says the directions.

Finally, there is a two-part written quiz. One girl quickly announces, "This is easy," as she matches numbered location names with a numbered map. She looks less confident as she examines the more difficult questions. Students must figure out a given continent by reading statements about its location in relation to other continents, for example, *"Yo vivo en _____ porque al oeste está Africa. Al noroeste está Asia. Al sur está Antártica"* (I live in _____ because to the west is Africa. To the northeast is Asia. To the south is Antarctica). Afterward, the class checks their work, reading the questions and answers aloud and sticking the correct numbers on the map at the front. There is time for a final rendition of the continents song and the teacher announces that next time they will turn their attention to a map of the United States.

The framework for this class and the other Spanish classes that Tarnowski teaches is the district's foreign language content-enriched curriculum, which is based on the district's overall curriculum content. "I have a general idea of what is going on in the other classes, and I try to match what they are doing," he says. "When that's not possible, I try to focus on what has the widest application or what has the highest interest to the children."

He also believes in the importance of reading Spanish. Even in third grade, the children can borrow Spanish books or magazines from the library. They also make their own booklets and do partner reading activities. "The main goal in these grades is speaking and comprehension, and there is certainly less writing than speaking," Tarnowski says. "But certain kids are visual learners, and we would be short-changing them if they were not exposed to print. In the early grades, I don't force the writing, but for those who want to, I let them go with it. In third grade and earlier, we do formulaic sorts of writing. Later on, in fourth through sixth grades, the children do more original writing."

His colleague, Jackie Pashko, a regular classroom teacher of third and fourth grade, agrees that the foreign language program is going well. "When this program was first introduced, I was somewhat ambivalent," Pashko says. "I thought of foreign language as a kind of enrichment for gifted children." Now she says that she recognizes how helpful the program is for all students. "It's an opportunity for these children to be rewarded for being verbal, another opportunity for them to shine," she says.

Lisa Pion, who teaches first and second grades at Sumner, agrees with Pashko. "There have been advantages [from their studying Spanish] with their learning to read and write English," she says. In her phonics program, she refers to the Spanish word *azul* and compares it with the English *school*. "It sounds similar, so we definitely talk about it," Pion says. She believes that the children are easily able to handle both languages.

Fifth Grade French at Armory Street School
Barbara Consolini's world language classroom at Armory Street School is full of props, posters, and charts in French and Spanish, and she teaches both. Books and games fill the shelves. The only

thing missing is a computer. Like Tarnowski, Consolini is the only language teacher in school.

Barbara Consolini's 30-minute French class for a group of 12 fifth graders goes smoothly. She uses French almost exclusively and awards stickers to children who do the same. Her lesson on animals of the forest is rich with pictures and figures of foxes, rabbits, squirrels, and other wild creatures. After 10 minutes reviewing a story the students had read previously, Consolini asks questions about various animals. Students look in their notes and consult a chart at the front of the room to help form their answers. Several stickers are awarded during the activity. The class concludes with the launching of a project. The students are going to make a book that compares a number of forest animals. Students collaborate with the teacher in making a diagram on the board, displaying the important information, especially similarities and differences, for l'ours (bear) and la chouette (owl). The 30 minutes go by quickly, and they will have to resume the book project next time. Students copy the chart and store the results in folders that they keep in the room.

Compared to lessons in Tarnowski's third grade class, this fifth-grade lesson shows a greater involvement with print and a bit more attention to accuracy, which is consistent with the district-wide curriculum. "I'm not really that concerned about grammar," Consolini says. "It's a gradual process, and I mostly want to expose them to as much language as I can. They already have the content foundation from the regular classroom teacher, so I can focus on the topics they like. They are generally motivated, and interest is high."

Angie Chaconas, a classroom teacher at Armory, is strongly supportive of the program. "It's one of the best things ever to happen to our school's curriculum, and I hope it is here to stay," she says. Chaconas observes that the children make connections from Spanish that help to improve their English vocabulary, and they become more confident in both languages. "I envy people who speak another language, " she says. "It's good that they're learning while still so young."

3.04 ■

Native Spanish Speakers Study Spanish

Both Sumner Avenue and Armory Street Schools have a large number of students whose home language is Spanish, which has turned out to be an asset to the language program. These children are sometimes used as Spanish classroom resources, providing Spanish vocabulary and cultural information to their classmates. In other classes, they often serve as translators for monolingual English-speaking classmates. Students from Spanish-speaking households usually profit from Spanish instruction as well, because they are generally familiar with informal spoken language and not so well acquainted with the more academic register taught at school (Valdés, 1995). Of course, some Spanish-speaking children simply study an unfamiliar language, such as French or Chinese.

Native Spanish Speakers

Articulation

Springfield has a history of foreign language instruction in elementary school that reaches back as far as the 1950s, when French was part of the curriculum for all fourth grade students. In the following decades, additional languages and other elementary grades were added. After the FLES program was all but eliminated during lean budget years in the 1980s, it re-emerged in the early 1990s, beginning to take its current structure in 1993, at least for a limited number of students (Riordan, 1998, pp. 263-264). The program became district-wide in 1995.

Perhaps it is partly because of this long history that articulation has been carefully built into the Springfield foreign language program. All students begin to study a language beginning in first grade, most often Spanish, though a number have a choice between French and Spanish, and a few have the option of Russian or Chinese. (Russian is available in a two-way immersion program at one K–8 school.) Students continue with their initial foreign language through fifth grade. In sixth grade, they can choose whether to continue with the language they are already studying or change to a different one. Riordan believes that offering this choice is particularly important since most children did not have a choice about which language to study earlier. About 65% of the children choose to stay with the language they started with.

All four of the languages offered in the elementary school program may be studied through Grade 12, according to the district plan. In order to accomplish this, "a number of logistical and instructional issues still need to be addressed," Riordan says. At present, only a few schools offer the less commonly taught languages, Russian and Chinese. After sixth grade, students stay within a sequential program in the language they have selected, but students in high school can add German, Italian, or Latin.

In addition to strong curricular guidelines, regular meetings support articulation among elementary grades and between elementary and higher grades. There are voluntary monthly meetings of all foreign language teachers, and workshops are held to bring together elementary and middle school instructional staff and principals. At these workshops, the teachers are able to develop a "sense of what is happening and what needs to be done" so they will be ready for the beginning of school the following September, Riordan says.

Assessment

FLES staff try to balance holistic and discrete-point assessments. On end-of-the-year speaking tests in eighth grade, for example, students are tape recorded as they respond to recorded speech prompts or to pictures, and teachers grade with a holistic rubric. Other tests rate students on their ability to carry out specific tasks, such as identifying objects in pictures or using appropriate greetings. The district-wide tests include listening comprehension in Grade 3 and tests of speaking and writing in Grades 8, 9, and 10. Teachers administer these tests and grade them using a holistic scoring system. To check accuracy, a 20% sample is spot checked by a committee, which gives a second rating. These ratings are shared with the teachers as a way for them to assess their own reliability as raters.

A third-grade listening comprehension test was developed for all four languages and is administered in all the schools. On this test, teachers read aloud 25 words and sentences from a standardized script, and students circle the picture that most closely matches what they hear.

Dozens of classroom assessment activities are used, as suggested in the curriculum frameworks documents. These range from oral interviews and presentations to reading comprehension assessment enhanced by visual cues.

The People Behind the Program
Foreign Language Teachers

William Tarnowski and Barbara Consolini, like nearly all other foreign language teachers in the FLES program, are certified for elementary school and are proficient in the languages they teach. One of the most important criteria during the hiring process is whether the applicant can actually speak the language. Partly because of Springfield's long involvement with foreign language instruction at the elementary level, most of the teachers are from the area. Other teachers have been recruited through advertising in newspapers, liaison with local colleges, and at meetings and conferences. "I never go anywhere without my flyers," says Kathleen Riordan. Word-of-mouth by current teachers has also been effective. For example, finding well-qualified Chinese instructors was not a problem, because the first teachers hired helped recruit new teachers. A challenge for Springfield is competing with more affluent districts in neighboring Connecticut for well-qualified teachers.

Parents

Parents are very supportive of the foreign language program, although their direct involvement is limited because most of them work. Parents learn about the program through school newsletters, a community cable network program that airs twice per month, school open houses, and parent/teacher conferences. But mostly they hear about it daily from their own children, especially when they bring home classwork in Spanish or French.

Gloria Smith, mother of Sumner students Jaleezah and Janet, says that this program is "right on time" for her daughters. "If they don't start until high school, it's too late, and learning the language would be really difficult," she says. Terry Benson, who has four children at Armory Street School, agrees. "When they are little they are aren't so shy or embarrassed just to jump in—and it probably sticks in their heads better."

Janine Fleet, whose daughter, Barbara, and son, Alex, study at Sumner, says that although neither she nor her husband speaks a foreign language, she is enthusiastic about their children learning Spanish. She observes that foreign language study trains the mind in a certain way and is useful in a career, but most important, "it enriches them as human beings and builds their respect for others." Fleet has been active in the Sumner Avenue School Parent/Teacher Organization, which has sponsored a Puerto Rican culture day and funded a recent Hispanic music presentation.

School Principals

Sumner Avenue School principal Carol Costigan says that her main role with the foreign language program is to ensure that it continues. She was the principal in 1993, when the schools were asked to implement the foreign language program. "I never needed converting," she says. "I think it contributes to brain development and overall learning."

Catherine McCarthy, principal of Armory Street School, is also supportive of the program. Knowing a foreign language is "beyond important and necessary," she says. "You're at a deficit without it." Because the Armory school attendance area includes both Spanish-speaking and historically French-speaking neighborhoods, both languages are offered at the school. Parents have been very enthusiastic, she says. "They have been requesting even more languages." But McCarthy's priority is to offer more support for foreign language activities after school. Possibilities include a Big Brother/Big Sister arrangement with high school students, volunteer tutors, or linkages with the YMCA and YWCA.

School Superintendent

Not all school principals have been as supportive as McCarthy and Costigan. When the program was first being implemented, a number of principals in the district were opposed, saying that time was being taken away from more important things and that the funds going to foreign language could be better allocated elsewhere. "They saw language learning as interfering with the development of other skills," says Peter Negroni, Superintendent of Springfield Public Schools.

Although Negroni is not responsible for the day-to-day operations of foreign language instruction in Springfield schools, many in the district say that his advocacy and leadership are largely responsible for the program's implementation and continuation. One big step has been that "the classroom teachers have come around" and now recognize the positive contribution that foreign language study has made in the language development of all students. "In a way, the traditional reputation of foreign language study has made it its own worst enemy," Negroni says. "There's been a perception that it is only for the most gifted." Negroni has been tireless in his support of foreign language instruction, once or twice having to tell a reluctant principal, "You will do this." He has also compromised when necessary, delaying the phasing in of foreign language instruction in kindergarten and first grade, for example, when a school wasn't quite ready to begin.

District Foreign Language Director

Kathleen Riordan's main areas of responsibility as Foreign Language Director for Springfield Public Schools are teacher recruitment, professional development, and curriculum development. She is quick to point out that she does not directly supervise the language teachers. "I visit the classes quite often," she says, "but not in an evaluative way unless there is a problem. It is the principals' responsibility to evaluate the teachers."

Riordan has been involved in foreign language teaching in Springfield for over 30 years. She taught Spanish and French at the junior high and high school levels before becoming the district's director for language programs in 1978. "It is all much more school-run than when I started," she says. Each school has its own budget for instructional materials, for example, and decides independently how to divide those funds among the subject areas. Although initial hiring decisions are made in the central district personnel office, if there are multiple candidates for a position in a school, the principal makes the choice.

Professional inservice development for language teachers is important, Riordan believes, and it must include both theory and practice. "People like to attend workshops that offer classroom strategies or 'make and take' materials they can use in their classrooms right away," she says. "But it is important to balance these with teachers' need for a better understanding of language acquisition. Understanding 'why' gives the practical things their value. Then the teacher knows how to fix an activity if it doesn't work as planned." She also insists that staff development focus on instructional goals. "Successful teaching is not just about activities," she points out. "The activities have to be more than busy work or fun; they must have a purpose."

Challenges

The Springfield FLES program faces a number of challenges, including the need for more after-school activities. Scheduling is a major challenge at most schools, because there is generally only one foreign language teacher for the entire school. Kathleen Riordan notes that it would be ideal if all schools could offer more time for language instruction. "If not enough time is devoted to language classes, then the students don't learn," and the program does not succeed. However, the ideal is not always possible, and providing adequate instructional time for all students in the school necessitates very creative scheduling of the foreign language teachers' time.

Assessment is a major concern, because funding is often contingent on test scores demonstrating success. Thus far, Springfield's foreign language program has fared well. Students are assessed on word, sentence, and paragraph recognition. They listen to spoken items and select a picture that best reflects the response for each item. Results show that students are demonstrating progress in listening comprehension, are mastering the vocabulary in the curriculum, and are beginning to internalize the language they hear in the classroom. Since 1998, a listening comprehension test has been administered to all third graders in the district. The biggest test of the FLES program will occur when the state language assessment is administered at a date as yet to be determined. The development of a state language assessment is the result of the addition of foreign languages to the state core curriculum.

Finally, the phasing in of two-way bilingual programs in many schools during the next few years will be a challenge. Successful implementation of one Russian and seven Spanish programs will require tremendous effort on a range of levels. The district intends to put a major focus on the professional development of teachers, the acquisition of appropriate instructional materials, and the education of parents for successful student recruitment and retention. As school board member Kenneth Shea points out, the board "has no issues with foreign language programs, but with bilingual programs, yes, there are political concerns."

Keys to Success

Two elements stand out as critical to the success of this ambitious district-wide program. Kathleen Riordan (1998, p. 266) says that flexibility is an important attribute for school and district staff who are initiating or implementing a foreign language program. She describes how important it is that school leaders and advocates recognize local realities and adapt to them. Springfield is a fine example of this flexibility, particularly since it has relied primarily on its own resources. Springfield is not a wealthy district, and its language programs benefit from few federally funded initiatives. However, it has used its limited funds creatively to support this well-organized program in a rather decentralized school system. The flexibility of the program is evident in the differences between schools, but the professional quality of the curriculum, content, and instruction testify to a core of high standards that all schools have agreed to.

The second key element of Springfield's success is leadership. "The best way to deal with diversity and culture is through language," Superintendent Peter Negroni stated in a video aired on Springfield's Channel 57 in 1997. "We believe that we are going to be the first district in the nation to graduate fully bilingual students in a variety of languages. And maybe, just maybe, they will know three or four languages." His enthusiasm is genuine and contagious. Like Negroni, Kathleen Riordan has been tireless, eloquent, and effective in her team building, her advocacy, and her efforts to make the program work. It is no mere coincidence that Springfield has such a well-designed foreign language curriculum and that Kathleen Riordan was tapped for Massachusetts's Foreign Languages Curriculum Development Committee. "When seeking advocates for language programs, one can never attend too many meetings, " she says (1998, p. 265). Riordan and Negroni have certainly done more than their share to ensure that the people of Springfield recognize foreign language learning as an integral part of public education.

Ephesus Road Elementary School

Chapel Hill–Carrboro City Schools
Chapel Hill, North Carolina

Huge student-painted murals decorate the classroom walls with scenes of the foothills, mountains, and coast of North Carolina. Twenty-one first graders are seated on the floor, listening, pointing, and repeating as the same number of fourth graders help them review French words for numbers, animals, colors, and verbs of motion. The fourth graders take turns asking questions in French about specific animals, such as, "Does it swim, or does it run?" and "Is it brown, or is it red?" Then the game begins. At the front of the room, eight numbered stuffed animals are sitting on chairs. A fourth grader pulls a numbered card from a sack and declares, "*Je vois, Je vois . . .*" ("I see, I see . . ."). And the younger children ask in French, "What do you see?" The fourth grader replies (in French) with hints: "It's an animal. It has four feet, it can walk, and it's brown." When a first grader guesses an animal (by number), a fourth grader holds up the stuffed representative for confirmation. Another fourth grader pulls another card and says, "I see, I see . . . I see an animal. . . . It has four feet, it can jump, it is green." And the six-year-olds guess the number indicating a frog.

The children describe and identify over a dozen stuffed animals with colors, shapes, body parts, and verbs of motion. The first-grade students are enchanted and extremely engaged. The fourth grade students are eager for their turn to participate and read descriptions in front of the class. When the game ends, there is a surprise. The fourth graders show the first graders a book they have written about the animals of North Carolina. It has already been presented to the school library, where it received official bar coding. All of the students are extremely proud. Language teachers Carol Orringer and Nathan Hester are also proud. This mixed-grade activity is the result of several weeks of planning and preparation for them and their students.

These students attend Ephesus Road Elementary School, the largest of seven elementary schools in Chapel Hill, a town in central North Carolina. The Chapel Hill–Carrboro City Schools have a districtwide enrollment of 8,227 in kindergarten through twelfth grade. Fourteen percent of the students qualify for the federally subsidized free lunch program. Students at the seven elementary schools participate in a content-enriched FLES program that was initiated district-wide in 1988-1989 in response to a state initiative. French is taught at three of the elementary schools, including Ephesus; Spanish is offered at the other four. Foreign language study is an option at all three middle schools and at the two high schools.

One of the fastest growing elementary schools in the district, Ephesus Road Elementary is a community-based neighborhood school with an enrollment of 686 students (1997-1998). All students participate in the foreign language program except those with severe developmental delays. The school's student population reflects the diversity of the community, with over 30 native languages represented.

Program Philosophy and Goals

"The program is not just 'Let's teach French,' " Carol Orringer says. "It's about multicultural understanding, appreciating differences, reminding students daily that people interact differently." Proficiency is the overall goal for the district's foreign language program. Students should be able to "communicate directly and effectively with people from other cultures" (Harris, 1998, p. 12). Three sub-goals support the overall language program goal of proficiency in listening, speaking, reading, writing, and culture.

1. Build cross-cultural understanding: The program emphasizes a positive attitude toward others, including those who come from other cultures. While learning the customs, cultures, and languages of other people, students learn how to live in an ever-changing society.
2. Develop communication skills: Students develop foreign language (called "world language" in program documentation) comprehension and expression. Instruction is carried out in the foreign language.
3. Incorporate grade-level and content-enriched curriculum: The World Language Program reinforces the grade-level curriculum through interdisciplinary activities. This is especially emphasized in Grades K–8. Content from other curricular areas is incorporated as much as possible.

(Harris, 1998, p. 12)

"These goals are for the entire district and for all grades, but the elementary program is the first step," says Carol Orringer.

Program History
Impetus
In 1985, the North Carolina legislature mandated that a North Carolina Standard Course of Study be developed that would make foreign language study a basic requirement in all elementary schools (Grades K–5) by 1993, with the option for students to continue foreign language study in Grades 6–12. The Chapel Hill–Carrboro City Schools system was one of the first in the state to adopt this plan, and funding enabled it to begin implementation by 1988.

4.01

Planning the Foreign Language Program

Prior to implementing a program, an advisory committee was formed to make recommendations to the local school board regarding the type of elementary foreign language program that should be offered and to develop a plan for implementing it. This advisory committee included parents, regular classroom teachers from the elementary, middle, and high schools, foreign language teachers from junior high and high school, principals, school district administrators, a liaison from the University of North Carolina (UNC) at Chapel Hill, world languages coordinators from two other counties, and a graduate intern from UNC–Chapel Hill. The committee conducted surveys, researched foreign language programs in other areas of the country, and conducted meetings with parents, school staff, and community members. Their recommendations included an overall plan for how the language program would be phased in and firmly established.

Planning the Foreign Language Program

Language Choice

French and Spanish were the two languages chosen to be taught in the districtwide elementary foreign language program, a decision based on the recommendations of the district's advisory committee. These languages were chosen because they would link to the foreign language instruction already provided in the middle schools, and because there was already expertise in French and Spanish within the district. In addition, because both Spanish and French are Romance languages, it was hoped that similarities between the two would facilitate the use of common teaching strategies and similar curricula and make it easier for students studying one language to learn the other language. To determine which schools should teach which languages, surveys were sent to elementary teachers, principals, and parents. French was chosen as the language of study at Ephesus Road Elementary School.

Initial Implementation

Because of the state mandate, the district had funding to appoint a foreign language teacher as a half-time coordinator to oversee the development and implementation of the program. Carol Orringer, now one of the two foreign language teachers at Ephesus Road Elementary School, held this position for 7 years during this early stage of program implementation. Before the program began operating, Orringer taught demonstration lessons in the elementary schools, which gave her the opportunity to build support and reduce apprehension about the program.

Orringer's responsibilities as coordinator included planning the curriculum. This involved incorporating state foreign language guidelines and integrating material from the regular elementary curriculum into the foreign language curriculum for a content-enriched approach. During her 7 years as coordinator, she met regularly with the elementary, middle, and high school foreign language teachers throughout the district, made presentations to the local school board, publicized the program, and continually looked for ways to improve it. The position was phased out when the FLES program became fully operational in all grades and state funding ended.

State Mandate Becomes Local Initiative

When it became apparent that the 1984 mandate would not be enforced as a law, many North Carolina districts dropped their plans for elementary foreign language programs. But the Chapel Hill–Carrboro City School district remained committed to the K–12 foreign language plan they had developed and begun to implement. They retained their elementary foreign language program with district funding, with state funding for the coordinator. At present, funding comes almost entirely from the district.

In the Classroom
Engaging Language Learning Activities

The French lessons at Ephesus Road Elementary School demonstrate that content-enriched instruction is not necessarily a dull, fact-drilling experience for the students. Even the learning objectives stated in the lesson plans indicate how lively and interesting the classes can be. For example, these are some of the objectives in Nathan Hester's plan for a fifth-grade lesson on the geography and time zones of Canada:

- Given an oral command, the students will move a cut-out of a moose, an animal native to Canada, in the correct direction on a map of the country.
- Based on the position of the moose, the students will identify in which geographic region of Canada the moose is traveling.

4.02 ■

French Class *(Grade 5)*
by Cassie Robertson and Megan Cullen
2/27/98

We enjoy French because it not only teaches French, but it teaches us about the world and our surroundings. To learn about these subjects in a fun way, we play games, sing songs, and make stories.

One thing we have learned about, is Canada. We have made a board game, that was about the races in Canada. It asked questions about Canada. During the second quarter of school, we learned about the regions in Canada. She taught us this by making a book about a moose that is looking for some leaves to eat and to do that he traveled into the 3 regions of Canada. The book said what was in each region. Then we made a small copy for ourselves.

- At the end of the moose's journey, the students will be able to tell what time it is in the new location of the moose (since the moose will travel through several time zones).

The lesson itself, conducted entirely in French, begins with a few warm-up questions about the time and date. Next, a student helper selected through a quick round of French hangman steps to the front, faces the class holding up a large clock and moves the hands, asking, "*Quelle heure est-il?*" (What time is it?). When Hester is satisfied that the students know their French time expressions, he asks about the times in different parts of Canada. "If it is 5 o'clock in British Columbia, what time is it in Quebec?" he asks, pointing to a large map. A geography review is next, accomplished through a group rendition of the familiar tune of "*La Cucaracha,*" but with French lyrics that list the provinces of Canada from west to east. Now the students are ready to listen to the teacher's story of the big moose that travels across the country to be reunited with its baby moose. Students sit in groups, each with its own map and moose figure. As the teacher narrates the rather farfetched tale, he punctuates the story with questions about the geographic regions and time zones that the moose gallops through. Hester checks that each group is able to position the moose correctly and that everyone can answer his questions. This part of the lesson ends with a math problem involving the local time where the moose began, the amount of time spent traveling, and the local time at the moose's destination. Hester circulates among the students to help individuals with any problems they may be having. The class closes with a song. During the entire activity-packed 20-minute lesson, not a word of English has been spoken, and the stated lesson objectives were definitely met.

No single methodology is followed by the teachers. "I'll use Total Physical Response or maybe a game, depending on the class," says Nathan Hester. "I try to select activities so that they follow a logical order, beginning with something easy so there will be a high success rate to build confidence, and then working toward the harder stuff." Hester also takes care to include a lot of visuals and "hands-on" activities in the lesson and builds in opportunities for students to volunteer. Although the teachers use French almost exclusively during the lessons, Carol Orringer says, "We make sure that the regular classroom teacher is clear on the lesson content and goals, and for that we use English."

Songs are a notable feature of the French program at Ephesus Road Elementary School. French teachers in the district have written and compiled collections of songs for students to sing in French. In addition to the Canadian geography song that Hester used in his lesson, there is also a "rap" for beginning a class, and songs about parts of the body, family relationships, clothing, and other basic topics. Content-based songs mostly focus on topics in science and geography, including temperature and weather, the planets, compass directions, and even the life cycle of the frog.

Students also write poetry. For example, students in one fifth-grade class wrote humorous poems about animals (see 4.03, "Les poèmes de Ryan Egan). In addition, students visit Web sites where they can read about French and read other students' work in French (see 4.04, "Ethnokids").

District-wide activities

Ephesus Road students participate in special system-wide programs and events such as the International Fair and Declamation Poetry Contest that bring the elementary, middle school, and high school programs together. "These types of activities are important and exciting," says Carol Orringer. "They help the teachers, administration, and students realize that they are all part of the same program, and they increase the chances that students will continue their involvement with languages as they advance through the system." In the annual Declamation Poetry Contest, elementary school students memorize and recite selected poems in their new language. A panel of three advanced foreign language students from the high school judges the presentations according to three criteria: knowledge of the poem, pronunciation, and quality of the presentation. The third criterion refers to whether the child seems to understand the poem and recites it with some feeling. A minimal participation fee is charged to cover the cost of the juice and certificates that everyone receives and the cost of prizes for the winners. Twenty-three Ephesus Road first graders participated in 1998.

Each spring an international fair is organized around a specific theme, such as "Many Places, Many Faces," and parents and others in the community attend. Each school in the district decorates a table or booth displaying student work and illustrating the cultures of the people who speak French, Spanish, and other languages. Ephesus students have the opportunity to make crêpes, show books they created, sing songs, and model costumes. A highlight of the

4.03 ■

Les poèmes de Ryan Egan
Je marche à minuit,
Je regarde les nuages.
Dans le grand ciel,
Je vois la lune de fromage!
. . . .
Je mange le déjeuner,
Vient le chien.
Le chien mange <u>mon</u> déjeuner,
Le chien dit, "Mmm. Très bien!"
. . . .
Il y a beaucoup d'animaux,
Dans la chaine alimentaire.
Qu'est-ce que mange l'unicorne?
Peut-être beaucoup d'air?
. . . .
Je marche dans ma maison,
J'écris à l'ordinateur,
L'ordinateur, il a faim,
Il mange l'ordinateur chip! J'ai peur!

4.04 ■

Ethnokids

A recent internet project of the French program at Ephesus Road Elementary is "Ethnokids" (http://www.ethnokids.net). This Web site is the joint effort of FLES program teachers and students at 14 elementary schools in 14 countries, including Belgium, Vietnam, Guyana, Romania, and Cote d'Ivoire. With all of its text in French, the site showcases the work of language learners between the ages of 9 and 11. When visitors select any one of the countries listed on the site, they see group photos of the children involved at the participating school, read brief essays the children have written, and see pictures the children have drawn. The students at Ephesus Road, for example, have not only written about their school, but also decorated a photograph "frame" with the

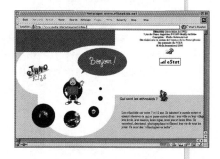

abbreviations "USA" and "NC" and with drawings of state symbols such as the cardinal, the boxwood turtle, the dogwood, and a carton of milk (the state beverage). Each school's contributions will eventually include "our celebrations," "our homes," and "our food." "Our Celebrations," the page for Ephesus Road, for example, features descriptive paragraphs about Halloween written by students Marianna and Christina. Students at the participating schools can use the site in a more interactive way by posting e-mail messages to one another. The Ethnokids site and its sections are under

continual development and revision by the schools involved and by the site's France-based proprietors.

festival is a World Languages poster contest. Three posters are chosen, one each from elementary, middle, and high school, and are displayed at the international fair. Both events are organized by Kathleen Rhodes, who teaches French at East Chapel Hill High School.

Curriculum
State guidelines
The French language curriculum at Ephesus Road Elementary reflects North Carolina state foreign language guidelines regarding areas of emphasis for elementary grades (North Carolina Department of Public Instruction, 1999). These guidelines, which have been revised several times during the life of the Chapel Hill program, are based on principles of child learning, the five Cs of the national foreign language standards, and the ACTFL proficiency guidelines (ACTFL, 1989). In kindergarten through second grade the focus is on listening, speaking, and cultural awareness, with a special emphasis on listening. "One must not forget that language acquisition begins with listening," the North Carolina guidelines point out (p. 36). Topics focus on the self, the home, and the school, and on content from other disciplines. Grammar is not explicitly taught, but it is not ignored either. The guidelines state that at at this age, children will acquire grammar most effectively "from context and when attention is given to function rather than terminology" (p. 37). In these earlier grades, culture is addressed in such competencies as using appropriate expressions and behavior in daily situations in the target culture. In addition, children are expected to "participate in activities related to major holidays, festivals, and special dates celebrated by children of the target culture" (p. 45). Foreign language reading and writing skills are not emphasized in first and second grades.

In Grades 3 through 5, the primary goal is for students to develop the ability to communicate purposefully, for example, to make and respond to requests. Students are expected to develop reading and writing skills as an extension of oral language, with an emphasis on pre-reading and pre-writing activities that "help students generate ideas, vocabulary, and structures needed to accomplish a task" (p. 47). Content area study expands in these grades to include the community and other parts of the world. For example, fifth-grade objectives for cultures include "demonstrat[ing] an awareness of the different target countries by locating them on a map or globe and identifying their major geographical features" and "identify[ing] people and products and their importance to the target cultures." In these grades, grammar is still approached indirectly in the context of communication activities. Teachers are encouraged to have students work in pairs and groups in the upper elementary years. Throughout the elementary grades, the North Carolina state guidelines recommend teaching strategies that emphasize "concrete situations accompanied by manipulatives and realia" and giving children the opportunity to move around the classroom (p. 48).

Curriculum revision

The elementary foreign language curricula for the Chapel Hill school district were drafted in the late 1980s and early 1990s as the program was developing. The K–12 foreign language curriculum was later aligned with local, state, and national standards. "Articulation, both across grade spans and from grade level to grade level, was undertaken to assure that students would receive a continuous and uniform instructional program from kindergarten to twelfth grade" (Harris, 1998, cover overleaf).

One result of this curriculum work has been a preliminary list of clearly stated exit outcomes for speaking, listening, reading, writing, and culture for each elementary grade level. These are shared across the district, so that students at Ephesus Road progress toward many of the same goals as their counterparts at the other elementary schools where French or Spanish is taught. This provides the opportunity for better articulation with the middle school language program as well.

4.05

French
(Grade 4)

This year in French we have learned how to count backwards, frontwards. We learned how to write (in French), how to read, how to do our ABC's, and how to name landscapes. We have also learned about French traditions. I have really enjoyed French this year and hope to continue.

By: Preston Smith (Grade 4)

The Five Cs

At Ephesus Road, the French program is so integrated into the rest of the school program that it is difficult to discuss the five Cs separately. For example, recently the early morning breakfast program in the school cafeteria was going well, so the assistant principal decided to treat the children to a French breakfast that involved setting the tables with tablecloths and flowers and offering foods such as croissants and fresh fruit. Word spread about the event, and the school declared an impromptu "French Day" as Carol Orringer and Nathan Hester scrambled to get posters up on the walls throughout the building. Orringer sent out an e-mail announcing the day, and soon the children were receiving best wishes for a successful French Day from all over the world. The event exemplified how a French program can include culture, communication, and community.

An effective way to include comparisons is when they arise natuarally. When students transfer from another school where they have studied Spanish, Ephesus Road language teachers seize the opportunity to compare languages and cultures. "We look at similarities and differences between French and Spanish," Orringer says. "In the process, everyone sees how Romance languages are similar to one another and different from English, and the newcomer gains confidence." Comparisons with English arise naturally as third graders write complete sentences in French describing themselves. "I ask questions about adjective placement and what letters are different in adjectives describing a girl and a boy (gender agreement)," says Nathan Hester.

Since the program is content-enriched, there are constant connections between French and the regular curriculum. In this program, one strategy to keep the connections flexible is "passing notes." The French teacher leaves a folder in the classroom where the regular teacher can leave a brief note, suggesting a topic that could be reinforced. When fourth graders were studying homophones in English lessons, for example, the note suggested that the children be asked to identify homophones in French. Other connections are more elaborate. Fifth graders who run the school store were required to learn about monetary conversion. They noted prices of all the items in the store and calculated what the prices would be in euros and francs. Later they held their own simulated market, complete with international currency made from poker chips and aluminum foil. A class of second graders who jogged daily decided to run from Chapel Hill to Paris in an imaginary way. They kept track of how far they ran each day and added everyone's miles together. When they reached their goal of 4,055 miles, they held a French celebration.

Articulation and Alignment

All elementary students in the Chapel Hill–Carrboro City School District have the opportunity to study foreign language (French or Spanish) in Grades K–12. Most Ephesus Road Elementary students proceed to Phillips Middle School, where they have the opportunity to continue their study of French. A curriculum for an articulated course at the middle school level was developed in 1994 for students with 3 or more years of French or Spanish at the elementary level. Still, there has been some controversy over the direction that the middle school foreign language curricula should take. Should the schools continue with a traditional middle school grammar-based curriculum that complements the oral communication focus at the elementary level? Or should the middle school program become more communicative? In any case, students of Spanish or French are able to continue studying the same language in middle school and high school in Chapel Hill.

Program Coordination Among Elementary Schools

Site-based management at the elementary level means that schools have more autonomy than they had previously, resulting in a wider range of delivery. For example, some schools, like Ephesus Road, may hold French lessons four days a week, whereas others may have somewhat longer lessons but only three days a week. Some schools offer foreign language to kindergarten students as an enrichment program, while others include kindergarteners in the regular foreign language instruction.

Although individual elementary schools have made changes in the frequency and duration of their foreign language class offerings, there is a great deal of collaboration, communication, and networking among all of the schools. The collaborative development of exit outcomes, for example, has brought the programs into closer alignment, as has the development of a system-wide test for foreign language students at the end of fifth grade.

Program Evaluation and Student Assessment

Student Assessment

In the elementary grades, the French classes use a four-point feedback system to indicate student progress. Teachers also keep a portfolio for each fourth- and fifth-grade student throughout the year. Students also evaluate themselves on their participation, listening, and writing using a four-point scale.

District-Wide Program Evaluation

After the elementary school component of the K–12 World Language Program had been in place for 5 years, a survey was conducted to assess the program's effectiveness. The survey was carried out in collaboration with Dr. Audrey L. Heining-Boynton (Heining-Boynton, 1990), a professor in the School of Education at the University of North Carolina at Chapel Hill, with grants from UNC–Chapel Hill and the U.S. Department of Education. Part of a longitudinal study of several districts, the study assessed the satisfaction and perceptions of the parents, classroom teachers, FLES teachers, administrators, and students. The results for the Chapel Hill schools were both positive and constructive.

Ninety-five percent of the parents surveyed were in favor of teaching foreign language to children at an early age. One parent commented, "Teaching a world language early enables a child to learn without the hesitancy or fear that one experiences at an older age." Regular classroom teachers were also supportive. Ninety-one percent responded that "the world language curriculum reinforces and enhances the topics they are covering." One teacher said, "The world language program is the best example of integration and active, hands-on learning in the school!" All of the teachers surveyed "agreed that their students are actively involved in their world language classes and enjoy this part of the day" (Harris, 1998, pp. 2-3).

Besides showing impressive support, survey results also indicated that parents wished to see more documentation of their children's learning. After focusing on the development of exit outcome statements in the 1995-96 school year, world language teachers and administrators in the district turned their attention to assessment of the students' progress. In the 1996-97 school year, they developed assessment instruments and procedures to determine the effectiveness of the world language curriculum and assess students' progress as world language learners.

At the elementary level, the testing program was designed for fifth graders. The end-of-year French test focuses on "aural comprehension, spoken language, pre-reading, pre-writing and some cultural awareness" (Harris, 1998, p. 16). As the students had not been given any formal tests in foreign language classes before, the regular and foreign language teachers practiced with the students on test-taking skills prior to the test administration in the spring of 1997.

4.06

A Special Relationship With the University

Audrey Heining-Boynton, the director of the foreign language teacher training program at the University of North Carolina at Chapel Hill, meets with Carol Orringer, one of Ephesus Road's language teachers, once a week. They talk about areas of mutual interest, possible program enhancements, and teaching tips. Heining-Boynton collaborates with the Ephesus Road teachers on conference presentations and workshops on content-based and content-enriched foreign language instruction. "There is a lot to be learned from the fun and joy that the kids have," Heining-Boynton says. The connection helps keep both the university teacher training program and the elementary foreign language program strong. Heining-Boynton commends Ephesus Road staff for their cooperativeness in working with student teachers. "Ephesus provides them with an excellent model and with opportunities for foreign language teaching, regardless of the student's language of concentration," she says. In addition to placing full-fledged student teachers at Ephesus Road, the university also sends education students to observe and to discover what it's like to start a school year. The university has given the school a reliable supply of well-qualified teachers, and the teachers are kept abreast of current trends in the field of foreign language teaching. The university was instrumental in conducting the program evaluation in 1994 that has led to enhancements in curricula and assessment systems.

The People Behind the Program
The Foreign Language Teachers

At Ephesus Road Elementary School, the two full-time foreign language teachers travel from room to room with instructional carts as they meet with 22 classes four times a week for 20 minutes. They work closely together as a team, with time set aside each week for joint planning, but they have separate offices where students can come for assistance or tutoring. Carol Orringer meets with the second grade, fourth grade, and most of the fifth grade classes. Her colleague, Nathan Hester, meets with all of the first and third grade classes and part of the fifth grade. Each visits 11 classrooms a day.

Carol Orringer also serves as a mentor for student teachers from the university who intern at the school each year. A seasoned foreign language professional with an MAT in French, Orringer is a frequent presenter at state and national professional conferences. In 1998, she was honored by the district as one of twelve Teachers of the Year. Orringer has appeared on local television several times, beginning with her introduction of the foreign language program to the community in the mid-1980s. Her work has also been noticed by *The Chapel Hill News*. A 1997 article (Tyson, 1997) describes her students concocting a gelatin reproduction of Claude Monet's painting of water lilies, a creative French twist on a lesson about solids, liquids, and gases.

Nathan Hester, a K–12 certified foreign language teacher, graduated from the University of North Carolina's teacher training program in 1997 after student teaching at the school the previous year. He joined the staff of Ephesus Road soon after he graduated. "I got my diploma on a Sunday and started teaching here on the following Monday," he recalls. He has quickly assumed a leadership role in the school, serving on the School Governance Committee since 1998.

The Regular Classroom Teachers

Hester and Orringer are well liked by teachers throughout the school. Because they travel from classroom to classroom, they have a natural opportunity to build relationships with the classroom teachers and to involve them in their instruction. The regular classroom teachers at Ephesus are very supportive of the foreign language program. They tend to stay in the classroom during the foreign language lessons in order to learn and then reinforce foreign language concepts during regular classroom instruction.

Annie Joines, a fourth and fifth grade teacher, believes that early language learning is important because young children have a good attitude toward it. "This is the time," Joines says. "The kids love it, they make mistakes, take risks, and learn an incredible amount of French! They know volumes more than high school students. They sing songs with complex French expressions and pronounce them correctly."

Joines gives the foreign language program credit for teaching children not to be intimidated by cultures and customs that are different from their own. "They could pick up and travel anywhere any time," Joines says. "They will always have an ease and comfort because of the foreign language program, and you don't get that if you wait until high school or college to start a foreign language!"

Joines says that having the foreign language teacher in her classroom almost every day helps them to coordinate instruction and strengthens regular instruction. She is able to talk with Orringer regularly. "We rarely go for more than two weeks without planning together," Joines says. She praises the foreign language teachers for their flexibility, such as postponing a planned lesson in order to seize an unexpected opportunity to reinforce a geology or social studies lesson. Classroom teachers feel that the foreign language program does not receive enough funding or enough time for instruction, Joines says. She believes that the teachers would support a program that met 5 times a week for 30 minutes and included kindergarten.

The Principal

The principal of Ephesus Road Elementary School, Terrence Young, has been involved with the program for over 4 years and has seen it grow. His role, he says, is to facilitate the recommendations made by the foreign language teachers. Young notes several features that contribute to the success of the program. One is the proximity to a university with an excellent teacher training program and student teachers. Another key feature, according to Young, is the coordination and cooperation of all the district elementary schools and the strong support of the parents and community. "No one in the district questions the value of foreign language in the elementary school," Young says. "Parents talk to me and are very pleased with and supportive of the program."

Terrence Young's vision for the program is to see its continued integration with the regular curriculum, helping the regular teachers to see that technology, science, and other areas can be integrated more fully with language instruction. He hopes that the program can expand, and that the regular classroom teachers can become more comfortable hearing and speaking the language.

At the District Level

The district's foreign language lead teacher, Kathleen Rhodes, is based at a Chapel Hill high school and has K–12 program coordination responsibilities in addition to a full teaching load. The lead teacher is responsible for communicating with the district foreign language teachers about program issues and for coordinating events that integrate the different school levels, notably the Declamation Poetry Contest and the International Fair and Poster Contest, in which foreign language students from across the district participate.

The district director of instruction K–12, Josephine Harris, is the liaison between the school and the district and between the district and the state. She is responsible for curricula, program planning, advocacy, classroom observations, support for new staff, and staff development. She meets monthly with the foreign language lead teacher and three to four times a year with the entire foreign language staff. She has responsibility for many curriculum areas, so foreign language makes up only a fraction of her multiple responsibilities.

From the very beginning, the local school board supported the state initiative to implement K–12 foreign language instruction, according to Neil Pedersen, Superintendent of Schools. "We believe strongly in the benefits of early language learning, and the board has never wavered in their commitment to the program," Pedersen says. The Ephesus Road Elementary School foreign language teachers have given presentations at school board meetings and regularly invite board members to observe and participate in foreign language classes.

The superintendent's vision is for a well-articulated K–12 program and an elementary program that grows regardless of students changing schools. He says this excellent, well-designed district program has always been strong at Ephesus Road Elementary, and that "the international flavor of the 'research triangle community' (an area that includes North Carolina State University, the University of North Carolina, and Duke University) creates an environment in which parents expect this type of program for their children."

Parents

"I try to be a hands-on kind of parent, " says Cindy Zwiacher, who has two children in Ephesus Road Elementary School and one who graduated the previous year. "I'm in touch with someone from the school at least once a week and with a foreign language teacher at least once a month." A past president of the school's PTA, Zwiacher finds many things to like about the foreign language program. "The early exposure is a huge benefit, and they do a really good job here," she says. "It's fun, interactive and hands-on." Her three children have participated in the Declamation Poetry contest, made lots of presentations, and participated in group projects. At home, they sometimes use French words at dinner, she says, and play games like "Geo Safari" using French cards. Zwiacher says that although French would not have been her first choice as a foreign language to learn, she is enthusiastic about foreign language learning in general. "I have never had a job where it wouldn't have been helpful," she says.

Parents play an important role in the school and in the FLES program. The PTA provides a great deal of support for the annual International Fair, supports the school newspaper, and contributes $150 to each teacher for instructional materials. At the International Fair, parents help with logistics and other aspects of the event. The foreign language teachers try to keep parents informed about school events, inviting them to attend classes, reporting on activities in newsletters, and working with them on the PTA and School Governance Committee. One parent who has visited classes writes, "It's fun to watch the students in (my son's) class perk up at 1:40 in the afternoon when Madame Orringer rolls her cart in and transports them to different cultures around the world. *Merci, Madame Orringer!*"

Students

Fourth grader Wendy Simmons had never studied a foreign language before when her family moved to the district in the middle of the school year, but she is enjoying the French lessons at Ephesus Road. "It's really different from my old school, but I like learning new stuff like a new language," Wendy says. "It's fun and it's interesting." Wendy reports that she isn't having much trouble keeping up. She doesn't participate orally as much as her more experienced classmates, but she doesn't mind asking questions when she doesn't understand. And Madame Orringer meets with her after school sometimes and has given her a videotape to watch at home. "It's fun to know something that Mom doesn't know," says Wendy.

Wendy's classmate Preston Smith has been studying French since first grade and had the opportunity to try out his language skills during a trip to France with his father last summer. "I was able to buy food, and wouldn't have been able to without using French," he says. On a train ride he was able to strike up a conversation about virtual pets with French children: *"Le bouton bleu, c'est manger"* (The blue button means eating). Preston is fond of real pets, too. "I have a dog, two cats, and three hamsters," he says, so his favorite unit in French is the one on the animals of North Carolina.

Preston and Wendy are not alone in their enthusiasm for French classes. One fifth grader, Henry Jicha, has been writing regularly (in English) about French class activities in the student newspaper since he was in third grade. His articles include a description of the Swiss celebration of *Escalade* and language activities to prepare for an up-coming district-wide language test for fifth graders. He concludes, "As you can see, this test is going to be relatively elaborate and official. However, we have smart kids at Ephesus. We won't have any trouble. . . . All in all this will be a pretty neat test to take. I am indeed looking forward to it and hope that you are too" (Jicha, 1997).

Challenges

One challenge identified by school principal Terrence Young is that a high rate of student turnover in the district's schools and redistricting efforts result in groups of students that lack the foreign language experience of their classmates. New students with little or no foreign language experience come to the school and join the classes of much more experienced foreign language learners. Some students transfer from a school that offers one language to a school that offers a different one.

Two other concerns, articulation and assessment, are being addressed through initiatives begun in 1994. As the middle school programs sort out methodology and curriculum issues, articulation with the elementary programs is improving. There is also a need to improve reading and writing instruction in the FLES program in order to bridge a gap between fifth and sixth grades.

In order to reliably determine the effectiveness of the foreign language curriculum and assess student progress, testing instruments are being revised annually. As the tests are brought into greater congruence with curricula, elementary grade exit criteria, and classroom instructional practices, they will more accurately reflect the accomplishments of the children.

Keys to Success

From the start there was a strong commitment from school staff and parents to the foreign language program in Chapel Hill. When reductions of the program were proposed, the community objected and won. Josephine Harris, the district's Director of Special Programs, wrote in her 1998 report that the district's foreign language program aimed "to move students beyond minimum compliance with state requirements" and set the goal of "developing functionally bilingual citizens" (Harris, 1998, p. 1). "The people in the community realize that it is not worth a lot of the district's money just to provide a 'taste' of a foreign language program," says Carol Orringer.

According to the district superintendent, Carol Orringer's early efforts were key: "to develop a well thought out plan that was supported financially and by the community." Principal Terrence Young says, "Carol did everything right. She built a base of support from the very beginning and continues to nurture it naturally, nearly unconsciously." As a result of Orringer's involvement, Young believes that it would be very difficult for anything to damage the program.

The strong relationship between the University of North Carolina at Chapel Hill and the program at Ephesus has contributed to the program's vitality and effectiveness. Because of the excellent teacher training program at the university, there is no shortage of well-trained K–12 certified foreign language teachers for the district's program. Because of numerous projects, meetings, and reciprocal arrangements with the university, Ephesus Road Elementary School receives the support and attention that help to make it a model for others.

Like most good programs, this one is continually evolving. The state guidelines and local curricula are just a starting point as Orringer and

Hester initiate Internet projects or find ways to add a French component to school initiatives and to reinforce regular classroom instruction. This is a program on the move!

Glastonbury Public Schools

Glastonbury, Connecticut

"Studying French in elementary school contributed to the kind of life I lead and the job that I hold today," wrote Richard Steffans, foreign service officer, during his 1995 tour of duty in Russia. "I certainly would never have gone to Russia had I not studied the language in Glastonbury" (quoted in Brown, 1995a, p.16). Steffans mentions a fellow Glastonbury graduate who was in charge of Federal Express operations in Moscow at that time. "She's a graduate of Glastonbury High School, and has a fantastic job in Russia that she couldn't have gotten without Russian language skills" (p. 16). Such testimonials from graduates are common in Glastonbury, Connecticut, where the public schools offer an articulated sequence of foreign language instruction from first grade through twelfth.

A Hartford suburb with a population of approximately 28,000, Glastonbury has been called "an average community" with a middle class income level (Christopher Cross in Brown, 1995a). But the Glastonbury Public School District's record of dedication to foreign language learning has been decidedly above average for a community of any size or income level. The foreign language program for elementary school students has been in place since 1957. Of the 6,000 students enrolled in Glastonbury Public Schools in 1999, 88% were Caucasian, and the remaining 12% were nearly equal numbers of Asian-American, Hispanic surnamed, and African-American students. Only 6% qualified for the free lunch program. At the middle and high school levels, nearly 15% of the students are studying two languages. "It's part of the town's culture," says Andrew Kyriacau, guidance counselor at Gideon Welles Middle School.

The foreign language program is implemented at all eight schools in the district. Spanish is taught to all students in Grades 1 through 5 at all five of the elementary schools. Sixth-grade students attend Academy School, where they make the transition to a more formal, academic study of Spanish or begin studying French. At Gideon Welles Middle School, seventh and eighth graders may continue with Spanish or French, or they may choose to begin studying Russian. Glastonbury High School offers not only these three languages, but Latin and Japanese as well. Classes meet 20 minutes twice per week in first grade, approximately 20 minutes per day in Grades 2 through 6, and 45 minutes a day in Grades 7 through 12. The addition of Japanese and the extension of the program to include first and second graders are among the more recent developments in this well-established program. Japanese is now offered to students from kindergarten through sixth grade at a magnet school that Glastonbury shares with East Hartford Public Schools.

Program Philosophy and Goals

Since the 1950s, all students in Glastonbury public schools have studied at least one foreign language beginning in elementary school. Initially funded through the National Defense Education Act in 1957, the FLES program in Glastonbury began as an effort to "take the Army language method and turn it into a program that could be used effectively throughout the nation" (Brown 1995a, p. 5). This federally funded project involved the development of curricula, materials, and instructional guidelines to support audio-lingual methodology in the public schools. Based on principles of behaviorist psychology, this methodology relies heavily on rote memorization of dialogs and mechanical drills and is no longer favored by applied linguists and language educators. Still, as Brown points out, the underlying purpose for adopting the methodology was "the need for Americans to *speak* other languages," rather than study the literature, which had previously dominated foreign language study (1995a, p. 6). This practical goal of communication has remained a central characteristic of the Glastonbury program throughout its history.

The four goals of the Glastonbury foreign language program today parallel national and state standards:

- To teach students to communicate beyond their native languages in order to participate effectively in the world.
- To enable students to recognize what is common to all human experience and to accept that which is different.
- To enhance students' ability to analyze, compare and contrast, synthesize, improvise, and examine cultures through a language and a perspective other than their own.
- To have students begin language study as early as possible in an interdisciplinary environment.

In the Classroom
Curriculum Integration
From first grade onward, the system-wide language curriculum integrates language instruction closely with social studies, mathematics, science, language arts, and art. Language arts themes are drawn from a language arts literature anthology used throughout the district. Other themes in the language classes reflect the district-wide social studies curricula and national geography standards.

These curriculum guidelines have led to thematic teaching units in which second graders, for example, learn about the history and geography of Mexico. "So far the students have learned about the great civilizations of the Olmecs, the Zapotecs, and the Mayas," writes teacher Monica Shuler. "They will also be learning about Teotihuacan and the Aztecs. . . . The students have also been learning traditional poems and songs of Mexico" (Shuler, 1997).

Fifth graders sometimes play a role in the second-grade unit on Mexico. Janet Asikainen, second-grade teacher at Eastbury School, says that fifth graders visit her class during this unit and teach the students Spanish numbers, names, and colors. "The children think of Spanish as a treat," she says (quoted in Brown, 1998, p. 11).

The integration with social studies continues through middle school and high school. Topics in the French curriculum include prehistory with a focus on the cave paintings at Lascaux (in Grade 7) and comparison between the French Revolution and the American Revolution (in Grade 8). The other languages taught in Glastonbury schools—Latin, Russian, and Japanese—are also integrated with content areas in the regular school curriculum.

For every grade level, the FLES curriculum includes goal statements for speaking, listening, reading, and writing based on the ACTFL Proficiency Guidelines (American Council on the Teaching of Foreign Languages, 1989). For example, this is the goal statement for reading in Grade 3:

> Children will begin to associate the spoken word with the written word. They will be able to identify isolated words and/or simple phrases when strongly supported by context. (Glastonbury Public Schools, 1999a)

For Glastonbury students, moving from Grade 5 to Grade 6 is an important transition in their language studies. At this time they choose whether to switch from Spanish to French for the next 3 years or to continue with Spanish. Either can be studied in a continuous sequence through twelfth grade. In sixth grade, language study becomes more formal, with some attention to grammar and the introduction of a textbook. However, the goal is still "to make the student a more proficient communicator" in the language, and teachers are encouraged to plan enjoyable, diverse activities related to the sixth-grade curriculum (Glastonbury Public Schools, 1999b).

The transition to using textbooks is somewhat challenging for students and the teachers. "Since they have been using authentic language all along," Christine Brown says, Glastonbury sixth graders "usually know the vocabulary [in introductory language text books], but the grammar is new." As a result, the curriculum suggests specific videos, periodicals, computer software programs, and supplemental textbooks to provide additional challenging learning materials for the students.

National Standards: Incorporating the 5 Cs

Beginning with Grade 6, Spanish learner goals and performance objectives are stated for each of the five Cs of the national foreign language standards (communication, cultures, community, comparisons, and connections). For each strand in the 1997-98 draft Spanish Grade Six Curriculum, there are one to three learner goal statements followed by up to 20 objectives. Under the heading "Community," for example, there are two goal statements:

- The students can use the language both within and beyond the school setting.
- The students can show evidence of becoming a life-long learner by using the language for personal enjoyment and enrichment.

Objectives under this heading include these:

- Students write and illustrate stories to present to others.
- Students perform for a school or community celebration.
- Students plan real or imaginary travel.

Engaging Language Learning Activities

After the 20 second graders have taken their seats in her classroom, Ida Shea's 20-minute Spanish lesson begins with a knock on the door. "*¿Quién es?*" "*¡Es Señora Shea!*" who asks typical greeting questions in Spanish as well as questions about the date and the weather. The children are eager to volunteer their answers. There follows a flashcard activity with the Spanish alphabet, then a spelling game.

Señora Shea spells words aloud in Spanish, and the students say the word. Next, she returns to questions, asking the children how old they are. All seem to be able to answer, and a few get silly, responding with "59" or answers in the hundreds and thousands. After a quick flashcard review of classroom vocabulary, the lesson moves to areas that have already been introduced in the regular classroom thematic unit on Mexico. Students try to identify geographical locations on a map, giving their names in Spanish: "*Rio Grande,*" "*Golfo de México,*" "*la Ciudad de México.*" Many are eager to volunteer, especially when a classmate gives a wrong answer. Before concluding the lesson with a vocabulary tic-tac-toe game, the students review song lyrics for a Mexican fiesta and sing it for the first time, with considerable success. "I take note of the regular curriculum and integrate the skills and content into the language lesson," Shea says. "Ten years ago, the lessons were mostly just conversational. This is much more meaningful to the kids."

Jean Despoteris, a Spanish teacher at Gideon Welles Middle School, decorates her classroom with student work, such as biographical timelines with photos, and fills the shelves with Spanish books, periodicals, and visual aids. Like her elementary school colleague, she begins the day's lesson by greeting the class of 22 eighth graders in Spanish and asking them about the date and the weather. Next, she asks what they did last night, reminding them to use the *preterito* verb form. After collecting homework paragraphs about their recent vacations, she reads a few aloud, asking the class to guess whose vacation is being described: "*¿Quién es?*" Most lesson activities are interactive and communicative but with a conscious integration of grammar points. There is a dual focus on form and meaning as Despoteris asks students about daily routines, using picture cues for waking up, eating breakfast, and doing homework. Their answers involve grammatical forms (reflexives) that they have studied previously. When a student asks a question or gives an answer in English, the teacher's response is in Spanish and seems to be understood.

The rest of the 45-minute lesson is about shopping. As with all of her other communication with the class, Despoteris gives activity directions in Spanish, though a few students share whispered English translations. After reviewing vocabulary sheets from the previous day, students take roles as shoppers and *vendedores* (sellers) and circulate around the room asking and answering questions about items for sale. After about 15 minutes of simulated shopping, pairs of students volunteer to demonstrate their ability to transact a sale in Spanish in front of the rest of the class. The lesson concludes with a commercial video featuring young people shopping at a market in a Spanish-speaking country. The students are clearly interested in the video and have little difficulty with their teacher's true/false questions about it afterward.

5.01

Foreign Language Week

During Foreign Language Week, all of the grades and all of the languages in the program are in the community spotlight. Elementary teachers hold demonstration foreign language lessons, which are very popular with parents and grandparents. A number even bring video cameras to preserve these moments for family video history. Parents and other community members come to see exhibits, sample foods, and watch student performances on International Night, when accomplishments of students at all grade levels are featured. Joseph Kiebish recalls one of his International Night experiences: "Groups in every language class put together displays about different foreign countries which included souvenirs, posters, and food." Lynn Campbell's Russian students also "had to research the culture and traditions of Latvia, Kazakhstan, Lithuania, Georgia, or another country and prepare a display in order to gain a deeper understanding of the former Soviet Union," Kiebish says (1999, p. 5). He also recalls participating in a display contest that served as a fund raiser to benefit an organization that helps women in Latin America. Between 500 and 800 people attend the Foreign Language Week events each year (Brown, 1995a).

Foreign Language Week

Articulation

The Glastonbury foreign language program is implemented district-wide, which includes all five elementary schools, the Academy School for Grade 6, Gideon Welles Middle School for Grades 7 and 8, and Glastonbury High School for Grades 9–12. The Glastonbury/East Hartford magnet elementary school is included as well. Articulation between grades and schools is supported by the detailed curricula and clearly stated goals for each grade. At each school, foreign language teachers work together as a team as they plan activities throughout the year. Not only do the foreign language teachers at each school communicate and coordinate with each other, but once a month all the foreign language teachers meet with the district's director of foreign languages to discuss curriculum issues and other district-wide priorities and activities. Assessment, for example, is planned collaboratively across languages and levels. "All textbook selection and curriculum design are undertaken by teachers representing elementary, middle, and high school," says Christine Brown (1995a, p. 12). "This type of planning ensures that students will move from level to level and build on skills rather than just repeating low-level skills at every stage of instruction."

One creative strategy for reinforcing articulation is exchange teaching. From time to time, the foreign language teachers trade classes: High school teachers move to an elementary school and vice versa. If an actual switch of teaching responsibilities is not possible, observations of each others' classes are arranged. This program has not only enhanced the continuity in the language program from one grade to the next, but has also encouraged teachers themselves to change schools. Ida Shea, a teacher at Buttonball Elementary School, for example, has taught Spanish in high school, sixth grade, middle school, and now second grade. "I really enjoyed sixth grade," she says, "as we start the transition to a more adult style of education, with textbooks and homework and so on—but this is the best." Another versatile instructor, Lynne Campbell, has enjoyed switching not only grade levels, but languages as well. A graduate of the Glastonbury program, Campbell studied Spanish in elementary school, added Russian in middle school, then French in high school. After further language study in college, she now teaches all three.

Christine Brown believes that if students begin a sequence of language study, the program "should not just drop them at some arbitrary point." In order to adhere to this standard, one seventh-grade Russian II class, for example, is held in the television laboratory at Gideon Welles Middle School, so that the teacher can reach level II students at the high school as well. In the elementary Japanese magnet program, a number of Glastonbury children attend school in East Hartford and begin learning Japanese in kindergarten. Brown says they will articulate the Japanese language program "not in a traditional format, but through the use of technology and distance learning strategies." At present, Japanese classes at Glastonbury High School use two-way video conferencing technology, which allows students at other area high schools and Manchester Community–Technical College to participate as well.

Articulation with post-secondary language programs is also a concern for the staff of Glastonbury Public Schools. A grant from the Modern Language Association is enabling the district to work with the University of Connecticut to enhance the high school to university transition for Glastonbury students who wish to continue their foreign language study. The collaboration will result in improved articulation of the entire local K–16 language curriculum and the alignment of assessment with instructional goals at all levels. Another result will be new professional development efforts for language teachers, focusing on second language acquisition, the national standards, standards-based implementation of technology into the curriculum, and improvements in the use of teacher and student portfolios throughout the sequence.

5.02 ▪

GOALS 2000

Since 1997, a Connecticut Goals 2000 grant project has enhanced professional development, interdisciplinary sharing, and networking among Glastonbury foreign language teachers and their non-language-teaching colleagues in elementary and middle schools. Summer workshops, a newsletter, and increased e-mail capability are strengthening articulation within the language program and promoting more integration with regular classroom instruction. For example, participating teachers have planned instructional units that integrate seventh graders' French lessons with the study of Egypt in social studies. An elementary school Spanish teacher is collaborating with an art teacher to develop units in which third graders use Spanish in oral descriptions of seascapes, and fifth graders write Spanish descriptions of portraits of relatives and friends. An additional highlight has been electronic linkage among the participating Glastonbury teachers and teachers in six other school districts.

GOALS 2000

Program Evaluation and Assessment of Student Achievement
Program Evaluation

Every 5 years the district conducts its own evaluation of the foreign language program. "We take a snapshot of the program and see if it is healthy," says Christine Brown. "Of course we look at state and national standards. We also look at such areas as which languages are offered, use of technology, and curriculum."

The 1995 program evaluation involved surveying current students, recent high school graduates, and parents of currently enrolled elementary students. Parents were asked about their own foreign language background and use as well as their perceptions of the language program and their children's language learning progress. They were invited to suggest additional languages to be included in the elementary program. Survey responses were reviewed by a 30-

member committee made up of teachers, school board members, guidance counselors, the director of the district's social studies program, school principals, and a number of community members. It was this evaluation, in part, that led to the expansion of the foreign language program from beginning in third grade to first grade.

Results of the evaluation also confirmed that Glastonbury's articulated sequence of foreign language instruction results in benefits for students who continue their language study. Glastonbury High School graduates generally compare their language proficiency very favorably to that of other students in their university classes. For the most part they placed "into the third semester language class at a minimum and the third year course at a maximum" at various universities (Brown 1995b, p. 3).

In 1986-87, Glastonbury students participated in the Connecticut Assessment of Educational Progress (Connecticut State Board of Education, 1987), a state-wide foreign language assessment that measured speaking, listening, reading, writing, and cultural knowledge. Approximately 1,000 Glastonbury students participated in this first-of-its-kind language testing of 26,000 students in Connecticut. Results showed that students who had started language study before Grade 4 outperformed students who had started language study in Grade 7 or 9 in all skill areas. Although the state has not been able to continue the testing, these compelling results have been used for the past decade in informational packets and presentations to the school board and the community as part of the rationale for continuing a strong FLES program.

Student Achievement

Portfolios document student progress in their foreign language learning from elementary grades through high school. Individual student portfolios include results from short-answer holistic exams (such as district-wide mid-year and final department exams), as well as from short-answer tests and quizzes (for grammar points), oral proficiency interviews, presentations, and student self-assessment.

Students' foreign language skills are assessed through formal tests, including the Glastonbury FLES Test (Thompson, 1997), beginning in Grade 5. Test instruments are devised, adopted, or adapted by a district-wide committee of language teachers and administrators. Brown wrote, "In these exams, students will listen to native speakers in real live situations, read articles from authentic sources, and write in responses to a real life event or activity. The teacher will conduct speaking interviews with students at all levels" (1995a, p.13).

Students' Views

In a 1985 survey of 1,200 Glastonbury High School graduates, many respondents cited the FLES program as their favorite component of their educational experience (Brown, 1998). Current students are also positive about the program, commenting on the challenge of learning a new language as well as how much fun the teachers are able to make it. Alice Lee, an eighth grader learning Russian in addition to Spanish, says, "There are tons of activities in Russian, like a version of Monopoly and the computer lab—not just lecturing." She especially appreciates that her teacher, Lynne Campbell, has introduced the students to symphonies and Russian ballet. Don Farrell, a classmate, mentions the Spanish Club as an extracurricular highlight for him. Both say that they mix the two languages up occasionally, and both are less comfortable using Russian than Spanish. "It's harder, and we have to be more serious," Alice says. Both report using Spanish outside school. "It's useful in traveling in the U.S.," Alice says. "When I was in Orlando and Tampa I was able to listen to a lot of people who didn't think I could understand what they were saying," Don says. Several Eastbury Elementary School students also say that foreign language knowledge will be useful if they ever travel abroad. "If you know a foreign language, you can also learn a lot about the country, people, and history of the language," one says (Brown, 1995a, p. 10).

Although he describes himself as hearing-impaired, former Glastonbury student Joseph Kiebish says that he is glad that the program does not separate students by ability. "Teachers took special interest in those who were eager to learn more, who had difficulty understanding a concept, or who needed a little bit more attention," he says. "It is important to include everyone in the experience," he says, adding that students were able to learn a great deal from one another (Kiebish, 1999, p. 3).

The People Behind the Program
The Foreign Language Teachers

In Grades 1 through 6, foreign language teachers have approximately 10 classes each day. The majority are assigned to a single school, but a few divide their time between two schools. In Grades 7 through 12, teachers have five 45-minute language classes daily.

The competence of these language teachers has been key to the success of the FLES program, according to Christine Brown, Glastonbury's director of foreign languages since 1983. This competence, she says, is not only in the languages, but in "their understanding of the broader curriculum" as well. Such teachers, Brown says, "form good relationships with the other classroom teachers and serve as general resources to the broader elementary school curriculum, especially in social studies" (Brown, 1995a, p. 11). Usually assigned to one school, the foreign language teachers in Glastonbury are better able to become part of that school's community than would an itinerant teacher.

Glastonbury's program has a good reputation and is able to attract well-qualified teachers. All of the teachers in the program are certified foreign language teachers, and most in Grades 1 through 6 have elementary certification as well. During the hiring process, Brown pre-screens candidates for all foreign language teaching positions to ensure that their linguistic and academic background and experience qualify them for the language teaching aspects of the job. All candidates are interviewed in the target language. Brown and the school principals then interview the finalists to determine how well the applicants will meet their school's specific needs. "This partnership has resulted in a stronger language program," Brown says. Newly hired teachers are observed and evaluated for 18 months to 4 years before becoming eligible for tenure. This process includes a mentoring program and a formal evaluation of the teacher's foreign language skills.

Graduates of the Glastonbury program have high praise for their language teachers, as Kiebish describes:

> They came into the classroom each day with the strong desire to teach and to make it enjoyable. It was not simply rote memorization of numerous vocabulary words, but a mixture of many different activities. One day it was flash cards, another day a movie. . . . Sometimes they brought in toy phones and we had "conversations" with classmates using the new words. They changed the way they taught so that it would continue to be fun and engaging. (1999, p. 3)

Foreign Language Director

As foreign language director for the entire district, Christine Brown is responsible for ensuring the quality of the program. She conducts about 90 classroom observations each year and oversees other formal program evaluation activities. In cooperation with the school principals, she ensures that teachers are meeting state-mandated teaching competencies, criteria for accreditation, and teacher evaluation. She works closely not only with the school principals, but also with all 42 foreign language teachers in the district. In addition to monthly department meetings with all of the foreign language teachers, Brown meets with each foreign language teacher about twice a year, first to formulate objectives, then to evaluate progress in meeting them. Students recognize her from her classroom visits, her work with parents, and her appearance at school assemblies when she helps fifth graders understand the language learning options that lie ahead of them. Much of the coordination and articulation among schools is due to Brown's efforts, both as an individual and as a team player with the teachers and school administrators. "Christy and her personality are definitely part of the program's success," says Andrew Kyriacau, a guidance counselor at Gideon Welles Middle School. "She is dynamic, a real advocate, and she hires people who are enthusiastic and work well with kids at this [middle school] level."

Although the foreign language program is funded primarily through the Glastonbury Public Schools, many of the program enhancements are the direct result of Brown's success at securing grants from state and federal sources. The Department of Defense funded the distance learning classrooms with video conferencing capability. The United States Information Agency has paid for foreign exchange student opportunities in the former Soviet Union. The Goals 2000 project was made possible by the state's Connecticut School Improvement Initiative funds. A Modern Language Association articulation grant is underwriting the project to improve articulation between the public schools' foreign language program and foreign language study at the University of Connecticut.

Brown is a strong advocate for linkage between the schools and the community. "Active, vocal, and well-informed parents can sway the opinions of unconvinced board members," she says (Brown, 1998, p. 8). Her office ensures that parents new to the district receive an information packet, including a student study guide and an audio tape about the foreign language program. A strong supporter of the district's Foreign Language Week and other local events, Brown has also helped publicize the program's accomplishments in talks at regional and national conferences and in articles published in professional journals for educators.

Despite this full load of district-level responsibilities, Brown also teaches one class of either Spanish or French each school year, "usually at the high school, depending on what the needs are, " she says. "It helps me ensure that articulation is on track, and it uses my background."

Parent Involvement: Travel, Field Trips, and Special Events

Parents are involved and active supporters of the foreign language program. "My daughter has been in the FLES program since she was in the third grade," says Marilyn Hamlin, who also teaches first grade. "Now that she is in the seventh grade, she has chosen to continue with Spanish and is thinking about Russian for high school. I feel the exposure to any foreign language at an early age can develop an awareness and appreciation of different cultures" (quoted in Brown, 1998, p. 9).

Parents contribute to the success of the program by monitoring their children's participation in distance learning projects; consulting with teachers about their youngsters' choice of languages for sixth grade; and serving as guest speakers, volunteer teacher aides, or tutors for Spanish or French. In a fourth-grade social studies unit on immigration, for example, parents acted as interviewers in an Ellis Island simulation. Other parents work with after-school activities, such as the French and Spanish Clubs, and serve as chaperones on trips, such as one that French language students took to Quebec. Many parents have hosted foreign exchange students from Latin America, Russia, and elsewhere. When the district budget cannot be stretched to support a worthwhile activity such as a travel or exchange program, parents have organized fund-raising events. In 1989, the Parent Teacher Organization and a parent volunteer group played an important part, with the district foreign language department, in raising funds for a remarkable student exchange program with the former Soviet Union. A dozen Glastonbury students visited Russia and Ukraine, and the same number of students from L'vov, Ukraine, visited Glastonbury.

Parent/Student Guide to Spanish in the Elementary Grades

One of the challenges facing all schools is that many students enter school in the district at the upper grades without the same preparation in earlier grades as their local peers. In the case of foreign lan-

5.03 ■

Helpful Hints for Incoming 6ᵗʰ Graders

For foreign language class Academy students need:
1 soft cover 3-ring binder
index cards (3x5 or 4x6)

Helpful hints:

1. Success will be in direct proportion to the amount of organized effort put into studying, reviewing, and practicing outside of class.

2. Be organized: Keep all handouts and worksheets in your foreign language notebook.

3. Do homework every day as assigned.

4. Be prepared to try, to take "risks," to participate in class activities. We learn a language by using the language.

5. Remember that short, simple answers are acceptable in the beginning foreign language classroom. Long or involved spoken responses or written answers will not be expected immediately.

6. Listen very carefully in class. It is not always necessary to understand absolutely every word, but to get the main idea of what is being said.

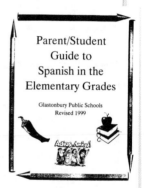

Parent/Student
Guide to
Spanish in the
Elementary Grades

Glastonbury Public Schools
Revised 1999

7. Students should practice new vocabulary, conversations, or questions and answers by reading them aloud. They could even teach this new language to another family member.

8. Make flashcards of new vocabulary words. Index cards can be cut into smaller 1-inch strips, English on one side, Spanish on the flip side. Parents, friends, and other family members can test the student's recall of vocabulary.

9. Practice new vocabulary by writing each word several times.

10. Practice at home! Volunteer and participate as much as possible in class!

Copyright © 1999 By Glastonbury Public Schools

guage programs, the problem is usually not just one of somewhat different content, as might be the case in language arts or science, but one of students having no background at all in the second language. Glastonbury has developed an interactive packet of materials to address this problem. New students and their parents receive a 45-page booklet and audio cassette, which provide language learning hints, an overview of Spanish pronunciation features, and dozens of interactive exercises that cover important language skills in the program. Though they focus primarily on vocabulary, there are also activities such as songs, designing a calendar in Spanish, and dressing a pair of cut-out paper figures following taped instructions in Spanish. The booklet includes a list of language learning resources that parents might investigate. These include dictionaries, computer programs, and one Web site (http://www.quia.com).

Board of Education

Like school boards in other districts, the Glastonbury Board of Education is primarily concerned with policy making and budgetary issues. When the district expanded the foreign language program to include first grade, the board had to consider the financial implications of the proposal. Unlike many boards though, the Glastonbury board not only supports the foreign language program, but also plays an active role in how it is implemented. The board takes part in curriculum reviews for all subjects on alternate years and has been active in the planned phasing in of technology, with a particular concern that teachers receive professional development so they can integrate technological resources and activities into their classes.

The Glastonbury Board of Education officially meets twice a month, but because of their involvement with such matters as curriculum review, they usually meet every week, says Suzanne Galvin, who was chair of the board for over 5 years. Galvin explains, "Kids sometimes come to the board meetings and talk about interesting foreign language trips they have taken, what they saw, did, and learned. Foreign languages are a central part of the curriculum. The world we live in is so global that foreign languages seem to be a necessity, a skill all students will need. It's important that they study other cultures."

Challenges

One of the challenges that the Glastonbury schools are tackling is articulation of their foreign language program with language study in higher education. "Our graduating students may find classrooms that are not proficiency-based," says Christine Brown. Students coming from a program that emphasizes spoken communication in the foreign language rather than literature may have a difficult time fitting in or finding a language program that meets their needs. As a result, "many of our graduates switch to another language and do well," Brown says.

Other ongoing challenges include the continuing need to identify and hire high-quality, experienced language teachers, continuing revision of curricula to integrate state and national standards, resolving scheduling difficulties, and strengthening the interdisciplinary aspects of the language program in all grades.

Keys to Success

The Glastonbury Public Schools foreign language program has many strengths. The program has a long, impressive history, many successful graduates, and committed staff. The program is responsive to student and community needs and incorporates state-of-the-art language teaching practices.

One program characteristic that stands out is its long, well-articulated course sequence, particularly in Spanish, but also in Russian and French—and soon in Japanese, as well. Articulation is accomplished through a coherent curriculum and assessment plan, teamwork within each school and across the district, inclusive curriculum planning processes, the innovative use of "exchange teaching," and enhancements provided through the Goals 2000 Project. The result has been a learning experience that leads graduates to make statements like that of Erin Doyle: "Studying Russian in grammar school was more than just another class for me. Literally my entire life has been shaped by that study" (Brown, 1995a, p. 14).

The other notable strength of the foreign language program in Glastonbury is the support it enjoys from just about everyone in town. Patricia Da Silva, principal of Buttonball Elementary School, says that Glastonbury was her first exposure to a FLES program. "I didn't seek a school with a foreign language program, but I was intrigued from the start," she says. "Before too long, I was proud to be a part of it. Acquisition of a foreign language pays off for all of us." Thomas Russo, principal of Gideon Welles Middle School, says the program is extremely popular, "the least controversial program in the school. The only problem is that there are so many opportunities but not enough time for students who want to take more foreign languages." Christine Brown does not take this widespread support for granted. She continues to educate parents and other community members and to win more advocates for the program. But she notes that she does not have to spend much time persuading the local government that early foreign language study is worthwhile. That support is more or less "built in," she says, "since many of the town council members went through the program themselves."

Andrew Jackson Middle School and Greenbelt Middle School

Prince George's County Public Schools, Maryland

Graduation from high school is traditionally the occasion for events such as dances, dinners, and parties, culminating in the formal school ceremony at which diplomas are awarded. But the most memorable graduation experience for 13 graduates of Central High School in Capital Heights, Maryland, may not be that cap-and-gown event. Their high school graduation was honored with a unique ceremony held at the Embassy of France in Washington, DC, on May 18, 1999. They received special certificates from Gladys Lipton, president of the American Association of Teachers of French, and personal congratulations from Jacques Bujon de L'Estang, the French Ambassador to the United States.

These 13 were the first students to complete all 13 years of Prince George's County School District's French immersion program. Comprised of programs at two elementary schools and two middle schools as well as Central High School, the program is one of very few in the United States to offer such an intensive, well-articulated language program.

Program Overview

Prince George's County School District, located on the urban fringe of Washington, DC, is the 17th largest in the nation. The district's K–12 school enrollment is 126,515 (1997-98): 70% African American, 20% Caucasian, 5% Spanish-surnamed, and 4% Asian American. There are 133 elementary schools (Grades K–6), 26 middle schools (Grades 7–8), and 22 high schools (Grades 9–12). Thirty percent of the students are eligible for free or reduced-cost lunch.

District-wide, 11,934 middle school students were studying a foreign language in 1997-1998 (Prince George's County Public Schools, 1998a). The average foreign language class size is between 25 and 30 students. Approximately 900 students participate each year in the K–8 French immersion program. Enrollment in the immersion program is on a lottery basis.

The French immersion program was established in 1986, beginning with kindergarten and first grade. Another grade was added each year. The middle school continuation program began in 1993 as the first students in the program graduated from elementary school. Andrew Jackson Middle School, already the site of a popular humanities magnet program in the town of District Heights, was selected for the foreign language immersion continuation program. The county's second middle school French immersion program began in 1997 at Greenbelt Middle School in Greenbelt, on the north side of the county. After middle school, students may continue foreign language immersion at Central High School in Capital Heights, which offers the International Baccalaureate program in addition to courses that build on the French immersion experience.

Whereas the elementary school program is total immersion, the continuation programs are, strictly speaking, partial immersion. In the elementary program, all but 2 hours of instruction per day—physical education and English language arts—are in French. In the middle and high school programs, it is the reverse: Most classes are in English, but 2 hours of each day involve content-based French instruction. Students take two bacK–to-back French classes, one in language arts and culture, the other in social studies.

The immersion programs are funded through the Prince George's County Schools and through the federal Magnet Schools Assistance Program. Magnet funding assists in the diversity of public schools by providing for innovative programs that will draw a diverse population to a particular school. Funding from the Magnet School Assistance Program is renewable annually.

Program Philosophy and Goals

Prince George's County Public Schools staff value foreign language study for its contribution to "communication, understanding other cultures, global perspectives, life enrichment, career enhancement, and expansion of the basic English vocabulary" (Prince George's County Public Schools, 1998a, p. i). The Prince George's County immersion program was founded on the belief that with intensive exposure to the language in a well-planned and monitored sequence of study, students will become bilingual and will demonstrate high academic achievement in the regular curriculum areas.

The immersion program has four goals for its students:

- They will learn the regular school curriculum through French.
- They will attain high academic standards.
- Their French language proficiency will approximate that of a native speaker by the end of sixth grade.
- Their skills and abilities will continue to approximate those of native French speakers at their respective age and grade levels as they progress through the program.

Starting the K–12 Program
Language of Choice

French was selected for the Prince George's County immersion program in the mid-1980s because of the existence of French immersion programs in Canada and in nearby Montgomery County, Maryland. Canada's French immersion model prescribes teaching the regular school curriculum through the medium of the foreign language rather than having foreign language be the subject of instruction. When skeptics in Prince George's County expressed doubts, immersion program advocates were able to point to the Canadian programs' success. Because a similar French program was already underway in Montgomery County, program developers in Prince George's County saw a potential local source for curricula and materials.

Starting the Middle School Program

As part of the middle school phase-in plan in the early 1990s, regular classroom teachers met with program planners to discuss curricula for reading, language arts, math, and science. They also discussed such questions as what should be covered in French and which French language textbooks should be selected. In addition, principals and instructional personnel met with parents and others who would be affected by the program to discuss the concept of immersion, special needs, scheduling concerns, staff development, library books, and supplementary materials. Budget concerns included funds for staffing, translation of curricula, materials, and consultant fees. An overview of the curriculum, *The French Immersion Program in the Middle School Curriculum Guide,* was updated in June 1999 and is available from the program.

In the Classroom

Madame Lundberg, an immersion teacher, begins her seventh-grade class at Andrew Jackson Middle School by informing students that for homework they are to draw a poster illustrating similarities among three religions. To ensure that students have understood the instructions, given entirely in French, she compares the word *similitude* to a word they already know, *similaire*, and then asks about *affiche* (poster). Students quickly state examples of items they might include on the poster: *eglise* (church), *temple* (temple), *mosquée* (mosque), *synagogue* (synagogue), and *prêtres* (priests), along with symbols such as *le croix* (the cross), *le croissant des étoiles* (star and crescent), and *l'étoile de David* (star of David).

Next, students review vocabulary related to religion while practicing different kinds of questions in several verb tenses. The teacher gives them a statement about cultural and religious information, and the students transform it into a question. Two points are awarded for an inversion question and one for a question beginning with *Que'est-ce que*. As they transform the teacher's statements into questions, students are learning facts about the religious customs and beliefs of those who practice Islam, Judaism, and Christianity. Afterward, a few of the students dress up in clothing worn by people who practice these religions, and the others grill them with such questions as, "*Pourquoi est-ce-que tu dois mettre cette voile?*" (Why do you have to wear that veil?) or "*Pourquoi est-ce que les femmes sont considerés inférieures?*" (Why are women considered inferior?) The student in costume responds to the questions appropriately. The lesson ends with a reminder about the homework assignment and a few more exercises on question forms for review.

This lesson, with its lively communicative activities, is typical of the immersion classes. Creative drama and role play are favorite activities among teachers and students alike. French immersion students complete ambitious interdisciplinary research projects in French on topics as diverse as Mozart, ancient Roman weapons and battle tactics, Elizabethan theater, and Pearl Harbor.

The immersion schools feature special programs and events, such as French essay contests (one of which is conducted by the French Embassy), in which the students have opportunities to display their language skills. Andrew Jackson Middle School has hosted a delegation from Senegal, sent immersion students to French-speaking areas of Canada, and held extracurricular foreign language camps.

In April 1998, seventh-grade immersion students from Greenbelt Middle School traveled to Louisiana to participate in an international festival in Lafayette. They also visited Pierre Part, Louisiana, where they were guests of French immersion students at the middle school there. A month later, the Pierre Part students visited the Washington, DC, area, and the Greenbelt students were able to repay their hospitality by hosting them for a White House tour and lunch at a local French restaurant.

In 1997, outreach efforts were initiated to connect the middle school students with those in the elementary and high school programs. The middle school students hosted student visitors from the elementary French immersion program and enjoyed receiving postcards in French when the high school immersion students traveled to France.

The Curriculum

As mentioned earlier, the French immersion middle school program consists of two daily courses taught in French: social studies and French language arts and culture. After bilingual instructors translated the district curricula into French, French history and literature texts and other materials were selected to implement the curricula. Whenever the regular social studies and language arts curricula are revised, the district foreign language office ensures that the foreign language curriculum is also revised accordingly. Because they are in the humanities magnet program, French immersion students write quarterly essays on an interdisciplinary theme or topic, conduct research, keep journals, discuss international topics, and may participate in field trips related to the themes being infused through English, social studies, and art. All students in the program are required to write a formal research paper each year. (See Prince George's County Public Schools, 1998b, for descriptions of the social studies and language arts curricula).

Social studies

The eastern hemisphere, past and present, is the focus of the seventh-grade social studies curriculum. Students learn about the continents of Africa, Europe, Asia, and Australia, with a regional focus on the Middle East. They study events within the same time period in these regions, with an emphasis on cultural differences and similarities. With the exception of Australia, students study each world region twice during the school year, first from a historical perspective and then a contemporary one. For example, when studying about Europe and Asia in the past, students read about myths and legends. In the unit on Europe in the contemporary time period, they read excerpts from a diary written by an adolescent female during the continuing struggle in Bosnia.

The eighth-grade social studies curriculum focuses on the history of the United States from 1776 to 1877, from the eve of the American revolution to the conclusion of the Civil War and Reconstruction. As with the seventh-grade course, teachers plan activities that promote hands-on experiences and presentation opportunities for students. "Students should be given exposure to significant pieces of literature and the study of primary source documents throughout the entire year" (Prince George's County Public Schools, 1998b, p. 15).

Curriculum and implementation suggestions are included in the district's "Social Studies Guide/Scope and Sequence." The core social studies textbooks are in French, and additional materials are translated into French or are adapted or created by the teacher or team of writers from the Foreign Language Office.

Language arts

In the language arts courses, students survey literature by reading literary works, social and cultural materials, and magazines and newspapers. Grammar is taught in context, and the finer points are analyzed as students complete writing assignments, original compositions, summaries, reports, and research activities.

6.01 ▪

National Standards in the Classroom

The national foreign language learning standards have been incorporated into the Prince George's County program curricula in all grades. The immersion teachers are aware of the standards and use the five strands in their instruction.

Communication in languages other than English: In addition to using French in the classroom for 2 hours every day, students use French when they go on foreign language field trips, in e-mail and regular mail exchanges with Canadian pen pals, at foreign language program events, and during travel overseas.

Connections with other disciplines and acquisition of information: In addition to learning about world studies in French, students study various literatures, art, and music in the French language. An interdisciplinary approach assures that what they learn in French during French language arts or world studies is integrated with what they are learning in English in other areas. An interdisciplinary exam requires the students to discuss and relate what they have learned in French and English on a range of specified topics.

Comparisons that develop insight into the nature of language and culture: The world studies curriculum and lessons include the comparison of French and English languages and French and American cultures. Comparison with many other languages and cultures is encouraged further through the study of various cultures in world studies and through exploratory and level I language offerings required in both seventh and eighth grade.

Knowledge and understanding of other cultures: The middle school world studies curriculum in both English and French focuses on learning about and understanding other world cultures and their histories, beliefs, and customs. Course content includes the cultures of various French-speaking countries as well as the cultures of other countries around the world, including Native American cultures and customs in the United States.

Participation in multilingual communities at home and around the world: Students participate in multilingual communities at school as they communicate with teachers from a number of countries. Locally, students are able to visit an authentic French restaurant where they place their orders in French. Students also take an international trip every summer to destinations that have included Japan, France, Spain, England, and Italy.

Teaching objectives for seventh and eighth grade include the following:

- Speaking/Listening: Students are able to express ideas clearly and concisely in a variety of oral contexts and to apply active listening skills to the analysis and evaluation of others' ideas.
- Reading/Literature: Students are able to decode, summarize, analyze, and evaluate works of fiction and non-fiction.
- Writing: Students are able to generate written communication in a variety of modes using all phases of the writing processes, including prewriting, drafting, editing, and publication.
- Language/Grammar: Students are able to understand and analyze the role of language in human communication and to apply correctly the conventions of standard French in both oral and written contexts.

(Prince George's County Public Schools, 1998b, pp. 1–8).

The curricula follow the Prince George's County School District guidelines, which are based on Maryland state guidelines. The Maryland School Performance Assessment Program (MSPAP) has also had a major impact on schools throughout the state as curricula and instruction are adjusted to enable students to meet standards as reflected by state test scores. At all levels, content in English and French is taught with MSPAP activities in mind. One middle school French teacher notes that language immersion strategies and MSPAP strategies in combination provide instruction that helps students to achieve a high level of foreign language proficiency and success on their MSPAP exams.

An Integrated Approach

In both seventh and eighth grade, world studies is part of an integrated approach that extends beyond the language and world studies classes. For example, when studying ancient Greece and Rome, students read Edith Hamilton's *Mythology* in English class and study ancient Greek and Roman art in fine arts class. Integrated assessment is carried out through quarterly essay exams. In addition, regular classroom teachers meet and chat informally with the foreign language immersion teachers to coordinate across disciplines. Integration involves deciding the content being covered as well as selecting complementary lessons, texts, materials, and tests. At Greenbelt Middle School, the foreign language teacher and English language arts teacher meet informally every few weeks to discuss ways to reinforce the material being covered in each class. Both are testing coordinators at the school, so these meetings give them opportunities to discuss interdisciplinary testing as well.

More Languages!

At both middle schools, seventh graders supplement their French study with the study of other languages in a foreign language exploratory course (FLEX). At Greenbelt Middle School, this course includes one semester of Russian and one semester that includes 2–4 weeks each of Latin, Spanish, and Japanese, and a unit on African languages and culture. At Andrew Jackson Middle School, the seventh grade FLEX course includes a one-semester sampling of Spanish, Japanese, and African languages and culture, and one semester of Japanese.

6.02 ∎

Exploratory Japanese

In a seventh-grade Japanese exploratory language class at Greenbelt Middle School, students look at three pictures: an eye, a heart, and a book, and decode them to mean, "I love books." The teacher, Maria Koulova, then asks them to draw a similar series of pictures to express a complete thought or idea, with no words allowed. After about 10 minutes of sketching on notebook paper, individual students volunteer to put their own pictures on the board at the front of the room while other students guess the meanings.

After discussing whether it is more difficult to represent a concrete object or an idea, students talk about why people need to write (e.g., to communicate with someone far away, to express feelings, to record history or events and achievements). This discussion leads to further illustrated explanations of the historical relationship between pictures and writing in Europe, North America, and West Africa. Next, the class focuses on the origins of the English language and alphabet, looking at the hieroglyphics of the ancient Egyptians and the alphabet of the ancient Greeks and Romans. Koulova points out that the Japanese similarly borrowed their writing from their closest neighbors, the Chinese. She explains that the *kanji* system, which is made up of over 10,000 characters, became difficult for the Japanese to use as the sole way to represent their language, leading to the development of two other writing systems, the *hiragana* and *katakana*. This prepares the class for watching a short video, "Japanese for Teens: Write in Japanese." Produced by Andrew Jackson Middle School, the video shows the (sometimes slight) resemblance between Japanese characters and what they represent. After the video, the teacher divides the class into small groups and distributes pictures that the students are asked to match with *kanji* cards. As assessment and closure, students write a sentence in their journals describing the *kanji* writing system and one character they learned that day. They also receive a *kanji* worksheet to complete as homework.

By the end of this lesson, the students may not have become more fluent or literate in Japanese, but they have met the lesson objectives:

• To describe *kanji* as a basic Japanese writing system.
• To explain why Japanese use more than one writing system.
• To recognize that writing systems are a reflection of the culture in which they are developed.
• To appreciate diversity, complexity, and logic in a writing system different from their own.

(Based on Sample Lesson Plan, developed by the district's foreign language office)

In the brief segments of the FLEX program, students are able to learn just a few simple expressions in each language, but they gain much more than a command of a handful of phrases. Looking at English word roots, prefixes, suffixes, and borrowed lexical items, they investigate the relationship between each of the languages and their own. In addition, they watch videos, carry out research projects, and enjoy presentations by visitors to become better acquainted with the cultures of the countries where these languages are spoken. The purpose of the FLEX program is for students to become more aware of the diversity of languages and cultures around the world, to develop additional language learning strategies, and to help them decide which foreign language might interest them for future formal study.

After seventh grade, the immersion students must study an additional language. Eighth graders at Greenbelt Middle School may take a year-long course in Spanish or Russian, while their counterparts at Andrew Jackson Middle School may take a year-long course in Spanish or Japanese. They may continue with these languages in an articulated sequence at Central High School.

The People Behind the Program

Close collaboration and cooperation among all those involved in the program have been vital to making this a well-articulated, successful immersion program. In addition to a foreign language supervisor at the district level who monitors the program and works with school principals, an immersion coordinator at each school handles the day-to-day operations of the program. A part-time foreign language immersion specialist provides staff development and program advice. Of course, it is the classroom teachers who provide the instruction.

Foreign Language Teachers

There is one foreign language immersion teacher at Andrew Jackson Middle School; there are two at Greenbelt. Each teacher has her own classroom and teaches two or three 2-hour foreign language blocks each day. All three teachers have both seventh- and eighth-grade students. The teachers have a 90-minute instructional planning period each day and a 30-minute break for lunch. In addition to teaching, teachers work with the foreign language supervisor and coordinators to develop the curriculum and to translate content-area curriculum units. At their home schools, they coordinate with each other and with the immersion and magnet coordinators regarding program issues.

The language expertise of the teachers is particularly important for immersion programs, because teachers must cover such sophisticated topics as literature, history, geography, and mythology. The Prince George's County teachers are native or near-native speakers of French and are trained in elementary or secondary education. All are fully qualified, either holding or completing their foreign language education certification. As of 1999, two of the three middle school immersion teachers had 10 or more years of foreign language teaching experience, most of it teaching elementary French immersion within the Prince George's County Public Schools.

Middle school immersion teachers participate in a variety of staff development activities each year, including courses from the University of Maryland/College Park and Bowie State University. These courses lead to certification for teachers of kindergarten through eighth grade. The district also offers staff development workshops. Recent workshops have focused on using technology in the foreign language classroom, incorporating national standards, and assessing students according to the ACTFL proficiency guidelines.

The District Foreign Language Supervisor

The district foreign language supervisor, Pat Barr-Harrison, plays multiple roles involving both leadership and support. She meets regularly with the magnet and immersion coordinators regarding program issues and visits the schools frequently to see that things are running smoothly. She holds workshops and meetings to address teachers' concerns, such as certification, articulation, and staff development. She coordinates curriculum development and translation and sees that those activities are funded. She devotes time to community relations and publicity for the program as well, issuing an annual newsletter, responding to inquiries from parents and community members, and meeting regularly with parent support groups.

The Principals

Decisions affecting the French immersion program are made by the principal and the district foreign language supervisor. The main role of the principal is to support the program and to ensure that all students achieve academic success. Recommendations regarding the program are made to the principals by the program staff so that the principal can take action and ensure that they are implemented. The principals of Andrew Jackson Middle School and Greenbelt Middle School are proponents of foreign language learning and strong supporters of the program.

The middle school program also enjoys support from the district school board, which views the entire K–12 immersion program as a success. Board members have made glowing statements about the program to *The Washington Post* and to reporters from French newspapers. Two board members have had their own children participate in the immersion program.

6.03 ■

Starting the Program at Greenbelt Middle School

In 1996, parents in the northern part of Prince George's County decided that they wanted the option of a nearby school where their children could continue to receive foreign language immersion instruction. A group of 16 parents addressed the principal of Greenbelt Middle School, asking him to join with them to advocate for a foreign language immersion program at that school. Parents and school administrators, with the help of the district foreign language coordinator, then convinced the school superintendent of the importance of this additional continuation program. It was implemented in 1997 and continues to expand.

Immersion Coordinators

"Immersion programs need special nurturing," says Pat Barr-Harrison. The immersion coordinators manage many of the day-to-day operations of the middle school program, helping it to run smoothly. They address curricular, student, teacher, school, and parent concerns and needs, and bring teachers' instructional concerns to the district foreign language supervisor. The coordinators meet with the teachers and with each other regularly to address program issues, and with the district foreign language supervisor to provide regular program updates.

The immersion coordinator assists the teachers by making sure that appropriate materials are available or ordered, helping with lesson plans, organizing special events and seminars for the students, and organizing special trips that involve the parents. Depending on student schedules from year to year, there may be as many as 20 field trips during a school year. "We use the District of Columbia as a classroom," says Corinne Mullen, immersion coordinator at Andrew Jackson Middle School.

Although teachers see her as a facilitator, students may view the immersion coordinator as a monitor. "No English in the French room," is a theme of Mullen's, and her job is to enforce the rules. Students are accustomed to hearing her exclaim, "*En français!*" when she catches them slipping into English. Repeated violations may result in phone calls to parents, detention, or other disciplinary action.

Middle school coordinators help to provide inservice training and contribute to the professional development of the teachers. At national conferences and within the district, they have delivered sessions on foreign language teaching and Maryland School Performance Assessment Program (MSPAP) strategies for new teachers.

Teams

Two on-going teams have proven to be an important asset to the program's continuity and community support. One team includes the district foreign language supervisor, the immersion coordinator from each school, the principals, the magnet coordinator, content area specialists, and parents. It was established in 1993 and meets once a month to discuss program concerns such as implementation, articulation, assessment and testing, and technology. Recent topic areas include aligning the curriculum with state standards and revising the French language arts course.

The second team consists of immersion teachers from both middle schools and meets periodically throughout the year to discuss the curriculum, assessment, technology, reading and communication skills, and other topics.

Parents

Parents are strong advocates of the immersion program at the middle schools and say that it is an excellent, challenging program that benefits their children academically, socially, and as citizens of a global society. They also believe that foreign language study contributes to job success and career advancement. "I wanted to broaden my daughter's horizons and give her an edge," one says. Another mother says that she had been nervous about putting her child in a French immersion environment, but her fears were dispelled as she saw how the children were succeeding in both English and French. She now says, "Children should start early in an immersion experience so that they can soak it up." Another parent noted that the test scores of students in the schools participating in the foreign language program are higher than those of students in the other district schools.

Parents are involved in a French immersion support group, the PTA, and school fund-raisers. A visiting delegation from Senegal was recently hosted by parents of children in the immersion program. A number of parents send their children to foreign language camp in the summer to maintain or improve their language skills.

Middle school parents say that their children are definitely using the foreign language at home. The youngsters read books in French, watch French videos, and read French menus or signs in restaurants. One parent says her child corresponds in French with Canadian pen pals, and others note that their children watch French programs on television. One parent mentioned that her child will recognize a French accent when someone is speaking and strike up a conversation.

Students
At both middle schools, foreign language immersion is an important feature that has attracted parents and children from outside the area neighborhoods. Students in the program are enthusiastic about it. "I really like learning things that are different from what everyone else is learning," says one.

Students use the foreign language in the classroom nearly all the time. They are encouraged to speak French outside the classroom, but this is not always convenient, because only a small percentage of the school population participates in the foreign language immersion program: 30 out of 910 students at Greenbelt, for example. Students are especially comfortable using the language with their immersion classmates. "French is handy to talk with friends (from the program) when we don't want our parents to understand what we're saying," one student says.

There are other opportunities outside the classroom for students to practice their French skills, including participating in the Canadian/ American exchange program and communicating with friends through an e-mail exchange. Immersion students are popular re-sources for others needing help in their regular middle school French classes. Although most middle school students do not participate in the program, immersion students report that there is no antagonism between the immersion and non-immersion students.

Funding

Funding for the foreign language immersion program comes from the district as well as from magnet desegregation funds, and is administered by the district foreign language office. Funding is one of the biggest challenges to the school and the district, but the district foreign language supervisor works to ensure that funds are available to maintain the immersion program that has served as a national model for many years.

The program coordinators and aide positions are supported by local funding that involves a position adjustment request with rationale. In the past, start-up costs were significant each year as a new grade was added to the program, involving the purchase of new instructional materials, translation of existing materials, and development of new curricula. Now that the program has been implemented in every grade from kindergarten through twelfth, expenses are for maintenance and enhancement. The amount of funding available through magnet desegregation sources has decreased as the program has completed its 13 years of implemention.

Measuring Program Success
Student Assessment

Assessments of student performance have validated the assumptions of parents and school staff that the French immersion program adds to students' capabilities in French and other subjects. Test score data collected for sixth-grade students at Rogers Heights Elementary School for the 1996-97 school year, for example, showed that these students were performing as well as or better than non-immersion students in English and mathematics on the Maryland state functional math and reading tests. The majority of the students also performed at or above average for their grade level on the various components of the Maryland School Performance Assessment Test, which measures hands-on problem solving in mathematics, science, reading, language usage, social studies, and writing. Results of a criterion-referenced French language test developed by the district indicate that French immersion students approximate native French speakers of the same age in a number of areas, including mastery of similar verb tenses, as well as in reading and writing tasks. It has been helpful to inform community leaders and parents of these test results. The Prince George's County Foreign Language Office shares successful evaluation results in program information packets that are distributed not only within the school system but also to parents and the general public.

Research reports and other written projects in middle school French classes provide a means of assessing students' writing skills. Peer revision is used to help students understand the writing process and become accustomed to editing, correcting, and assessing their own work. Oral presentations also provide a means of assessing general oral proficiency and identifying strengths and weaknesses in such areas as content, word choice, tone, and projection. One teacher uses the Maryland School Performance Assessment Program rubric for grading and has the students assess themselves and their peers using this system. Students compare the grades they give themselves with those given by the teacher. Much of a student's grade is based on classwork and oral participation.

Portfolios are maintained for each student so that their work can be shared with high school teachers as an important element of program articulation. Teachers also share assessment results across grade levels and refer to them when they examine the scope and sequence of the program each year to determine whether the outcomes are still appropriate.

Program Evaluation

In 1996, the Center for Applied Linguistics conducted an extensive evaluation of the French immersion program in Grades K–8. This evaluation included 64 classroom observations, reviews of over 250 weekly lesson plans, staff interviews, and surveys of teachers, students, and parents. The results were quite positive.

The study confirmed that immersion instruction was implemented as planned. Content areas such as mathematics, science, and language arts were being covered in French, and the MSPAP activities were included as part of instruction. Perhaps the most significant finding was that the students in the immersion program were acquiring skills in French that enabled them to communicate with native speakers of French through both speaking and writing. Evaluation of speaking and writing samples from third, sixth, and eighth graders revealed that the program was meeting the speaking and writing objectives set forth in its scope and sequence (Center for Applied Linguistics, 1997).

Linking the Program to Families and the Community

The district foreign language office provides a variety of informational materials, pamphlets, and brochures about the multiple foreign language offerings in the Prince George's County school system: talented and gifted, foreign language exploratory, foreign language immersion, foreign language in the elementary school, and dual language enrichment. The materials include instructional program overviews, descriptions, goals and histories. There are recommended guidelines; expectations and offerings at various grade levels; and scope and sequence with outcomes and indicators for listening, speaking, reading, and writing in a foreign language.

The district foreign language supervisor combines reports from the French immersion and magnet school coordinators to produce a district French immersion newsletter to inform school administrators, parents, and the community of the accomplishments of the foreign language immersion students and staff. The newsletter includes statistical information, such as the results of consecutive year enrollment studies, as well as descriptions of activities and special events such as research projects, field trips, and visits from foreign diplomats.

6.04 ■

"Bonjour"  "Ça Va?"

French Immersion
June 1999 Newsletter

Dr. Pat Barr-Harrison
Supervisor of Foreign Languages
Prince George's County Public Schools

Information

A special thank you to all parents who interacted with teachers, administrators, and other parents to make learning in an immersion setting a **positive experience for students.**

This year ended with **a positive "Bang"** due to the publicity about "**The First 12th grade** **Graduating Immersion Class"** in Prince George's County; the other highlight was **Rogers Heights** and Shadyside having 1st Place winners **and honors** in the **National** French Contest. Imogen Davidson White took **first place** in the U.S. on the exam in her category. Imogen will be a sixth grade immersion student next year taking advanced courses in math and other subjects. **Hats-Off** to **Imogen** and all of the other students.

A special **thank you to the Immersion teachers** and the **five French Immersion Coordinators** in the five Immersion Schools. They work with me, the principal and you to make the program in Prince George's County Public Schools **(PGCPS) one of the best in the U.S.**

Every year I ask teachers and coordinators to highlight special activities or an event to share with parents, other teachers, students, and other stakeholders in the Immersion Program. In addition, I have added some information from the Internet. Please enjoy the Newsletter.

Like other classroom teachers, the teachers in the immersion program keep in touch with parents through regular phone calls, progress reports, and quarterly conferences. Parents are welcome to sit in on classes to observe, and a number of them do so each year. There are also special programs and plays held during or after school, and special events such as a recent visit from a representative of the Japanese embassy. Parents develop a strong pride in their children's accomplishments as they are involved in these events.

The district's public relations office publicizes the program's success in the area newspapers. For example, in 1997 and 1999, local newspapers published articles about Prince George's County immersion students scoring top in the nation on "*Le Grand Concours de Français*" (The National French Exam) administered yearly by the American Association of Teachers of French. A student from one of the immersion elementary schools had the top score in the nation in 1997, and another in 1999. *The Washington Post* featured an article in May 1999 about the first graduates to complete the immersion program's K–12 sequence (Nakamura, 1999).

Challenges

Despite overall success, the immersion program is not without its issues and challenges. Although the retention rate from elementary to middle school is over 95%, the retention rate from middle school to high school is not as impressive. Ninety percent of Andrew Jackson Middle School immersion students continue with the program in high school, but fewer than 50% of Greenbelt students do so. One of the main reasons is that Central High School is not in a convenient location for students living in the northern part of this large district.

Transportation is a related challenge. Because of the size of the school district, a number of immersion students in all grades must travel considerable distances to participate. When the district's transportation budget is tightened, immersion students and their parents are directly affected.

6.05 ■

Students in a rigorous Prince George's French program greet well-wishers after a ceremony at the French Embassy. From left are Reginald Andrews Jr., Heavenly Hicks, Aliesha Sharpe, Kelea Bosse, Kimberly Webb, Lajeral Churchwell and Ainsley Delissaint.

BY DAYNA SMITH—THE WASHINGTON POST

Bilingual Honors for Bilingual Students

Pr. George's Seniors End 13-Year Program With Ceremony at French Embassy

By DAVID NAKAMURA
Washington Post Staff Writer

Reginald Andrews Jr. is a star running back at Central High School in Capitol Heights, and he's not a bad wrestler, either. But the skills that really win him attention among his peers are strictly verbal: He speaks French.

Take the time he was working in a McDonald's last summer and a group of foreign tourists was baffled by the nuances of the quarterpounder with cheese.

"I said, *'Est-ce que je peux vous aidez?'* " Andrews recalled yesterday. "Just asking them if I could help them in French made them feel better. My co-workers were shocked."

Andrews, a senior, and a dozen of his classmates were honored at the French Embassy in Washington yesterday as the first students in the mid-Atlantic region to complete a K-12 bilingual program, emerging fluent in both French and English.

The Prince George's French immersion program, offered at two elementary schools, two middle schools and Central High, is one of the most advanced language programs in the country. While many school districts, including Montgomery and Fairfax, offer language programs in elementary schools, Prince George's is one of the few on the East Coast that offers a continuous and comprehensive bilingual education from kindergarten through 12th grade.

"This shows how immersion works: that these people, who for 13 years studied in French, are now fluent," said Dominique Malicet, the French Embassy's cultural attache. "And in a world where everybody talks about globalization, they're already ahead."

The Prince George's immersion program was one of several magnet programs developed by the county in the late 1980s, when the school system was inventing ways to foster the voluntary integration of schools.

Jonis Belu-John remembers his mother anxiously camping out all night so she could sign him up. He also remembers his own reaction being less enthusiastic.

"The first year, I was in awe," he said. "I was like, 'What is this? Why am I here? Why can't I speak English like everyone else is doing in their classes?' But I picked it up pretty well because that's all we spoke, French."

Isabella Rouse enrolled her daughter, Donna Jackson, in the program after looking into the science and math magnet schools.

"They got more exposure, traveled, did things you do not usually do in school," Rouse said of the immersion program. "I wanted a lot of diverse things for her, and this program did that."

In the program, elementary students are taught the standard American curriculum in French for most of the day—the exceptions being gym class and English literature. In middle school and high school, students learn reading, writing, science and math in English, but take two periods of social sciences in French.

Sometimes, the students said yesterday, it was a daunting task to keep up.

Ainsley Delissaint, whose French-speaking father signed him up for the immersion program, said he started doubting whether he'd be able to keep up when he reached middle school and some of his original classmates dropped out of the program.

"My parents said it was my decision," Delissaint said. "I finally decided that I've been in there so long, it didn't seem right for me to jump. . . . I had prepared for this since kindergarten."

Most of the students' parents chose to start them in the program. But at the middle and high school levels, they made their own decisions to stick with it.

As they grew older, students said, they began to appreciate their ability through a standard high school measuring stick: peer reaction.

"My friends always say, 'You should say something in French to me,' " Aliesha Sharpe said. "I say, 'Why? Y'all are not going to understand what I'm saying.' But they think it's good because they take French 1 and 2 and they don't get anywhere."

Belu-John, whose younger brother also is in the county's French immersion program, uses his fluency to his advantage—sometimes to his parents' chagrin.

"My brother and I, whenever we want to talk about my parents, we make comments in French and they can't understand us," Belu-John, who plans to major in international business and aspires to be a diplomat, said with a grin.

As for Andrews, he plans to major in business and start a restaurant—possibly an international chain.

He figures his language skills will come in handy, even if the most popular menu item is a Big Mac. "There's no translation for that," Andrews said. "That's a pretty universal concept."

A third challenge is class size—26 to 30 students per class. This is done to accommodate as many students as possible. But the development of speaking skills, in particular, can suffer with so many students in one class. This challenges teachers to plan lesson activities that provide maximum opportunity for students to practice speaking French.

Keys to Success

Three elements stand out as essential to the success of the Prince George's County immersion program. The first is the support that the program enjoys from just about everyone. The program is appreciated by parents, who are amazed to hear their children speaking only French in the classroom. Parents believe this is an enormous opportunity for their children and, along with journalists, often make appointments to visit and observe. Program staff have not had to expend time or energy convincing skeptical school board members. Impressed with test results, the board has supported the program from the start. According to the principal of Greenbelt Middle School, there have been no complaints from anyone since the program started.

Another key to the program's success has been long-range planning. Because the program was conceived from the beginning as a K–12 sequence, articulation has been part of the planning and implementation from the start. The program has, for the most part, avoided the problems of inconsistent teaching approaches or curriculum gaps that can diminish effectiveness.

The third element that has contributed to program success is teacher commitment to the students and to the immersion program goals. Teachers spend extra time not only planning lessons, but also doing curriculum work, participating in staff development, and communicating with the community. "They feel valued by the program, so they give a lot to it," says Pat Barr-Harrison.

Larchmont Elementary School

Toledo Public Schools, Toledo, Ohio

When María Elena Martínez wheels her materials cart into the classroom at 1:00 p.m. on Wednesday, Sylvia Boyd and her 26 second graders know that they will not hear or speak a word of English for the next half hour. Today Martínez begins by pulling a variety of colorful plastic fruits and vegetables from a grab bag. She holds up each one asking questions in Spanish: *¿Que es, fruta o verdura?* (fruit or vegetable?). *¿Que color es?* (What color is it?). *¿Que es?* (What is it?). A few of the children peek at a worksheet from Monday's lesson to check on the Spanish words for fruits and vegetables; others glance at the Spanish color chart on a bulletin board. Martínez strolls around the room repeating her questions and passing out tokens to students who answer correctly. The tokens are part of a rewards/assessment system she uses in place of grades. Next there is a brief activity in which students tell her how many fruits and vegetables she is pulling from the bag. Then Martínez asks a boy to show her *dos verduras* (two vegetables). When he points at the celery and a cucumber, she asks the other students, *"¿Bien o mal?" "¡Bien!"* they chorus, so she hands the boy a token. Classroom teacher Sylvia Boyd specifically requested an arithmetic focus this week, so by the end of the lesson students are working on addition and subtraction problems in Spanish.

Program Overview

Maria Martínez's half-hour Spanish lesson for this second-grade class is typical of the content-enriched foreign language lessons at three elementary schools in Toledo, Ohio: Larchmont Elementary School (Spanish), Arlington Elementary (French), and Keyser Elementary (German). All three have the same program design, relying on a single foreign language teacher to provide content-enriched lessons twice a week to students in Grades 1 through 6.

Toledo is a large urban school district serving nearly 40,000 students at 43 elementary schools, 8 junior high schools, and 7 high schools. The student body at Larchmont Elementary School is ethnically less diverse than many other schools in the district. Only 11% of Larchmont's students are African American, for example, whereas African Americans comprise 41% of the total student population in the district. Approximately 330 students attend Larchmont, most of them walking to school from homes in the neighborhood. The principal, Jeffrey Hanthorn, describes the neighborhood as "middle class, majority blue collar, with a minority population that is ever growing, which is to the school's benefit." Hanthorn says that the percentage of students eligible for free and reduced-price lunch also continues to increase.

Program Philosophy and Goals

This is the philosophy behind the program:

All children who can function in their first language have the capacity to function at that same level in a second language. Instruction in a second language at the onset of formal education is important in order to produce linguistically-aware and culturally-tolerant individuals who will contribute to our nation's effectiveness in global issues.

Students in the program are expected to achieve the following goals:

- Engage in second language activities designed to reinforce, re-mediate, and enrich grade level objectives in the district's course of study in math, science, and social studies.
- Develop listening skills to function in age-appropriate activities.
- Develop novice-level oral proficiency skills in vocabulary areas basic to their age and interests.
- Develop limited reading and writing skills in the second language. *(Toledo Public Schools, 1997)*

Principal Hanthorn cautions that the goal of the program is not bilingualism. "At the end of sixth grade, the children will not be holding conversations with native speakers," he says. However, he points out, the program offers many benefits for the children, including "exposure to another language, understanding of different cultures, reinforcement of course content, and a more native-like Spanish accent." The program focuses on communicative activities and developing a strong foundation for future language study.

History

The Toledo Public Schools initiated this content-enriched FLES (foreign language in elementary school) program in 1992 following the recommendation of a district-level elementary foreign language committee. All of the elementary schools in the district were surveyed to find out which of them supported the idea of early foreign language instruction and were interested in implementing a FLES program. School principals and the teachers' union had a role in making decisions that shaped the program. The decision was made to offer a different language (Spanish, French, German) at each of three schools.

The program began with foreign language instruction in first grade only. One grade per year was added at all three schools, completing the sequence with implementation at the sixth grade level in 1997. Kindergarten was not included, because it is only a half-day program. Funding from a state grant helped pay for foreign language teachers during the first 3 years, but district funding has been relied on since then. "We needed to make the Spanish instructor a full-time position when we reached Grade 4 a few years ago," recalls Hanthorn, "and there was total support at the school and district levels." In addition to teachers' salaries, district funds pay for curriculum development and some supplies, such as the foreign language editions of *Scholastic News.*

In the Classroom

María Martínez begins this third-grade class with a *buenos días* song, then holds up a large, labeled picture of a sunflower from *Scholastic News en Español.* Referring to the picture, she introduces plant-related vocabulary in Spanish without translating into English: seeds, leaves, roots, stem, flower, and petals. Martínez checks on pronunciation as students read and repeat the vocabulary from a handout. Next she introduces the growth process of a plant, using Total Physical Response. The students first watch and then imitate as she pantomimes the life of a plant—crouching as a seed, wiggling fingers to indicate being watered, receiving sunlight with outstretched arms, and then growing toward the sun. They participate first as a whole group, then pairs come forward to demonstrate. The children clearly enjoy learning the vocabulary and reviewing the science concepts in this physical way. Before the class ends, the students read and circle correct answers to such questions as "*¿Cuál es la flor más alta?*" (Which flower is tallest?) by referring to a height chart comparing different types of flowers (*Scholastic News,* April 1998, edition 1). An *adiós* song ends the half-hour lesson.

Maria Martínez's teaching skills are at the center of the content-enriched Spanish program at Larchmont Elementary School. Because there are no textbooks, and she is the only Spanish teacher for all six grades, she creates all of the lessons and tailors them to meet the needs of different classes. The lesson described above, for example, is completely different from one she did for another class of third graders the day before, because that group is studying tadpoles and frogs, and their teacher requested an emphasis on arithmetic. In the early years of the program, Martínez also had to translate texts and create a lot of her own materials. "Now there are quite a few good Spanish materials available commercially," she says, citing the T.S. Denison *Segundo Grado* worksheets as an example.

Martínez exchanges information with the classroom teachers after the foreign language lesson and encourages them to provide information about what they plan to cover in class each week so that she can integrate their priorities with the Spanish curriculum. Because she is busy covering so many different classes, this information is conveyed on a simple form rather than in a face-to-face meeting.

7.01

DEAR TEACHERS:

      IN ORDER TO MEET THE OBJECTIVE(S) OF REINFORCING THE CURRICULUM IN SPANISH I WOULD LIKE TO REQUEST THAT YOU FILL OUT THE FOLLOWING FORM.

GRADE _3_   WEEK OF _April 20, 1998_

TEACHER _Mrs. Cunningham_

THESE ARE SOME OF THE THINGS WE WILL BE DOING IN:

SOCIAL STUDIES _Transportation_

MATH _Multiplication and division facts_
They're not doing so well. They are not retaining it
well except for Tony, Rashid, Cheryl

SCIENCE _Classifying Living Things_

                            THANK YOU / GRACIAS,

                            MARIA ELENA MARTINEZ

Content form

The lessons all take place in the regular classrooms, with the regular classroom teacher observing or participating in a support role. Martínez is conscientious about using only Spanish during the foreign language class periods. In fact, during the second year of the program, when she whispered something in English to the regular classroom teacher after the lesson, one of the second graders overheard her and became excited. He turned to a classmate saying, "Did you know that she speaks English?" Martínez had taught the boy for a year in the first grade without his hearing her use any English at all! The students are instructed to use only Spanish as well, and Martínez encourages this by awarding points that can be used in the *Mercado* activity (see 7.02) at the end of the year.

Martínez meets with her first class at Larchmont at 9:25 a.m. and finishes her final adiós song of the day at 2:55 p.m. She meets with 11 classes twice a week, five to seven groups each day. She has a one-hour break for lunch and lesson planning every day and some additional planning time at various times each day. Like the art teacher, Martínez has a desk and storage space for an instructional materials cart in the teacher lounge, where she spends her planning time. Much of her additional planning and materials preparation are done at home. On Fridays, Martínez works on language curriculum, materials, and assessment at the International Studies Center.

Because the Spanish lessons are brief and are held only twice per week, reinforcing the lesson content is important. Martínez says that there is "spiral reviewing" of the material from first through sixth grades so that students retain much of what is introduced. "We cover some of the same areas several times," she says, "things like dinosaurs, animals in various areas, the five senses, cultural events, and cities and states. We have to keep reviewing so they won't forget." In addition, because they stay through the language lessons, regular classroom teachers can reinforce Spanish vocabulary during their own lessons. Occasionally they ask Martínez to provide Spanish labels for their science or social studies bulletin boards.

7.02

Mercado de Artesanía

María Martínez assesses student participation and oral proficiency throughout the year by awarding *puntos* (points) that are exchanged for imitation pesos to be used to purchase food, arts, and crafts at the end-of-year *mercado de artesanía* (arts and crafts market). By adding up students' points, Martínez can get a good idea of how much they participate and also of how proficient they are. Any student who attempts an answer is awarded a point, but additional points are awarded to a student who has pronounced something particularly well, used more complicated language and vocabulary, longer sentences, or correct grammar. Extra points are awarded for doing homework, giving oral reports, or creating posters. Students also gain points if they take classwork home and read it to parents, who sign a statement saying, "My son/daughter has read to me the following (report, work)." This reinforces classwork and keeps parents informed of what their child is learning.

The *mercado de artesanía* is held the last few days of school. Students create their own arts and crafts to sell, as authentic and multicultural as possible. Typical items include masks, friendship bracelets, bookmarks, clay pots, maracas, piñatas, and paper-mâché fruit. This approach is fun and motivating for the students, says Martínez. "Students are excited about buying things at the market, but don't feel pressure to receive a certain number of points or a particular grade."

Mercado de Artesanía

Teaching techniques associated with the Natural Approach and Whole Language Approach to reading are favored by Martínez and her colleagues at the two other schools with content-enriched FLES programs. Grammar is introduced in Grades 5 and 6. "We encourage students to correct their own errors whenever possible," Martínez says. "They learn better that way."

7.03 ■

Edible Incentives for Participation

If every student in a class participates on a given day, everyone has handed in assignments, and no one has misbehaved, the entire class receives a star. When a class has earned 10 stars they receive a special reward, usually involving food. The class will have a special cooking activity preparing traditional food, such as Mexican hot chocolate or *buñuelos*. Not only do they learn to prepare the food and eat it, but they also sing songs about the food and learn about native ingredients and traditional food preparation equipment. Martínez says that there are very few behavior problems in her language classes. Intent on earning stars and points for the *mercado*, her students pay attention, behave, and participate. "If you want to learn a language, you must participate," Martínez says.

■

Curriculum

The curriculum was developed by a team of teachers and school administrators who met weekly during the initial years of program implementation. Following the content stipulated in the district's plan for instruction, the team developed FLES program and content area objectives for first through sixth grades. These are grouped into the following categories:

- Mathematics
- Cultural knowledge
- Multidisciplinary connections, information, and knowledge
- Science
- Insights into the nature of language and culture
- Social studies

Specific learning outcomes are suggested for each category at each grade level. These are examples of objectives for fifth graders in the category of multidisciplinary connections, information, and knowledge:

- Use map skills.
- Use grid system and compass to locate places.
- Interpret and analyze maps, charts, and graphs to formulate geographic ideas.
- Describe geographic conditions in the target countries.
- Write simple responses to messages, texts, and letters.

The curriculum is consistent with the Ohio Model Curriculum published in 1996, which is itself based on current national standards and ACTFL guidelines. The students at Larchmont and the other two elementary schools are expected to "function in Stage One activities" as described in the state curriculum. The district's overview booklet states, "After successful completion of the FLES program, Grade 1–6 students' language acquisition skills should have progressed from mechanical utterances to communicative activities. They should progress to Stage Two activities in junior high or high school." María Martínez and former district foreign language director Lori Winne both served on the advisory committee that contributed to the development of the state model curriculum.

The People Behind the Program
The Foreign Language Teacher

Maria Martínez has been bilingual for as long as she can remember. Her father was born in Toledo but raised in Mexico City. He and her grandmother spoke Spanish at home and insisted that she speak only Spanish with them. With a B.A. in elementary education and an M.A. in Spanish, Martínez brings an impressive level of professionalism to the Toledo program. She has taught for over 20 years in the Toledo Public Schools, serving in 10 different schools and handling assignments as varied as high school Outward Bound and kindergarten ESL. She says that being bilingual helps her to adjust to changes in the lesson requested by the regular classroom teacher: "I can go into the classroom and wing it, adapt and go with it."

Lori Winne, the district director of foreign language instruction through 1999, says that Martínez has developed strong professional relationships with most of the classroom teachers in the school. "Teachers give up bulletin board space for the language," she notes. As the regular classroom teachers become more familiar with what Martínez can do, they ask her to introduce new concepts to the children, not just reinforce what they have already studied. "Then they will begin the next lesson by asking, 'Do you remember what *Señora* did yesterday?' " says Winne. They also ask Martínez for Spanish language worksheets that students can work on when they finish other tasks early and have extra time.

Martínez has been with the Toledo FLES program since it began, serving on the foreign language committee with the school principal prior to program implementation. She also played an important role in training the first French and German teachers in the program, since they were experienced only in secondary school language teaching. She still works with them on use of manipulatives, pictures, cut-outs, and flannel boards. She is a frequent presenter at state and national professional conferences.

The Regular Classroom Teachers

Regular classroom teachers at all three schools are very supportive of the FLES program. "It (foreign language skill) is important for students to be able to compete in the world today," says one teacher. Others add that foreign language study "increases awareness of other cultures" and "helps to eliminate ethnocentricity."

These teachers say that the FLES program enhances regular classroom instruction. They know this firsthand, because they are in the classroom for all language lessons. Although it is difficult for them to find time to meet one-on-one with Martínez, they fill out the weekly content form to tell her what to emphasize, and this has worked well. "She really does adapt quickly to what we want," says one teacher, recalling a time when she mentioned to Martínez just before class that she was doing a special unit on states, and Martínez included vocabulary that was relevant to the new unit.

The teachers say that the content-enriched instruction supports the regular curriculum, allowing the students "to see the same thing in a different light." The reinforcement of multiplication and division facts is one example; new science kits with English explanations on one side and Spanish on the reverse side are another. The Spanish teacher reinforces science, social studies, and math through thematic units on topics like butterflies, dinosaurs, and plants. The regular teachers also try to incorporate Spanish in their instruction, using Spanish words and numbers themselves or having the children give Spanish equivalents.

The classroom teachers say that it is good that the program is not graded. "The students pick up the language so easily and that is good for their self esteem," they say. They would like to see the Spanish program expand to the junior high feeder school.

The Principal

Jeffrey Hanthorn, principal at Larchmont Elementary since 1986, is extremely supportive of foreign language instruction and welcomed it at the school. Involved in the program since its inception, he has picked up a great deal of Spanish himself, "though I understand much more than I can speak." He says that his main roles are to support the teachers and to provide structure, control, and discipline, so that the children know they must always be on good behavior. He visits the classrooms regularly, sometimes using Spanish phrases he has learned with the students. Hanthorn says that it is important for children to know that there are people with other languages and cultures who have interests and problems similar to their own. As a result, he has supported the hosting of foreign exchange students at Larchmont. Hanthorn has also been known to bring Larchmont students to meetings of the district board of education to demonstrate the effectiveness of the Spanish language instruction they receive.

The District Foreign Language Supervisor

Lori Winne was the Director of Foreign Languages for Toledo Public Schools through 1999. It is largely due to Winne's vision and initiative that the foreign language program began. Impressed with research that showed children's success at learning foreign languages, Winne wrote the grant proposal that resulted in the initial funding to launch the program, headed the committee that developed the program, and oversaw the start-up.

She says that the program has come a long way since it began in 1992. In the first year, two of the teachers were drawn from the secondary school instructional staff. "They had never taught younger children," she recalls, "so we started out by having them go to the schools and observe regular elementary classes." During the summer before the program began, Winne designed and directed an intensive two-week teacher preparation program, including a foreign language camp experience held in the district administrative offices. "In the morning the teachers taught language lessons to the children and were videotaped," Winne says. "Then they critiqued themselves and one another in the afternoon." Though current teachers in the program have a stronger background in elementary education, the two-week mini-camp is still offered each summer. "The opportunity for practice and peer critique is invaluable as in-service training," Winne says.

7.04 ▪

International Studies Center

Using funds from a federal FLAP (Foreign Language Assistance Program) grant, Toledo Public Schools established the International Studies Center in 1992, converting the second floor of an old hotel building into classrooms, offices, and multi-media rooms. Since 1993, the International Studies Center has provided instruction to children and adults in over 10 different languages. Until 1998, many of the children were from private schools, but now the center also provides foreign language instruction for interested middle school students from the public schools. Since 1999, interested sixth graders from the FLES program schools may attend as well. Lori Winne estimates that about a fourth of eligible students attend.

The Center offers a Saturday morning foreign language program for elementary students based on fairy tales and on math, science, and social studies activities. Winne and Martínez developed versions of the curriculum for six languages. In addition to language classes, the center teaches geography and social studies and offers teleconference facilities and a sophisticated multi-media lab. The facilities are open weekends and evenings as well as weekdays during the regular school year, and during summer months as well.

International Studies Center

Parents

"I really believe in foreign language learning at an early age," says Jane Nickerson, a pre-school teacher whose son is a sixth grader at Larchmont. Greg Carr, father of a second grader and a sixth grader, agrees. "It's a multilingual world," he says, noting the linguistic diversity in Toledo, Detroit, and other U.S. communities. "And Spanish is the fastest growing language and the fastest growing ethnic group in this country," he points out. According to these parents, the activities that encourage their children with foreign language learning are regular homework, the market project (*mercado de artesanía*), and computers. They know that their children use the language outside class, "but not with their parents," says Nickerson. Her son has a friend who speaks several languages, "and he thinks that's fascinating," she says. Carr says that his two children sometimes use their Spanish with one another.

Parents Nickerson and Carr are in contact with those responsible for the foreign language program, either the foreign language teacher or the principal, at least once a month. They participate in foreign language and school programs by volunteering and by fundraising for field trips and special projects. They say their children really enjoy the Spanish classes. "They love the market project—and they learned to do the Macarena before anyone else had even heard of it," Nickerson says.

Students

"A few days ago I got an autograph from a Cuban baseball player and surprised him by speaking Spanish," says Sean, a sixth grader at Larchmont. Like Sean, Stephanie, a fifth grader, has been in the FLES program since first grade and enjoys it very much. "I like the plays, even the rehearsing," she says, referring to a Spanish version of "The Three Little Pigs" that the fifth and sixth graders put on for the other students. The two students appreciate the patience and creativity that Señora Martínez brings to the Spanish lessons. "She explains if we have questions, she tells us to practice and doesn't get angry—and sometimes she helps kids after school," they say. They both enjoy winning points for the end-of-year market activity but also appreciate other things: tapes with alphabet and songs, books in Spanish in a section of the library, special foods (e.g., *buñuelos,* deep-fried flour tortillas sprinkled with sugar), and doing the Macarena and the Mexican Hat Dance. Sean and Stephanie agree that Spanish language skills will help them communicate with Spanish speakers who visit Toledo or whom they meet if they travel, but first of all, "It's really going to help in high school."

Program Evaluation and Assessment of Student Achievement
Student Assessment

In addition to awarding students *mercado* points, Martínez keeps portfolios from second through sixth grade to show student progress each year. These portfolios will be shared with the middle school or high school teachers to show what the students have already accomplished and what they are ready to tackle at the next level.

End-of-year formal assessments have been conducted in fourth, fifth, and sixth grades, and there are plans to add a speaking and listening component in the earlier grades as well. The fourth-grade assessments, administered after 100 hours of instruction, cover reading, writing, listening, and speaking. Reading and writing activities include recognition of common vocabulary, sentence comprehension, and classification of fruits and vegetables. The word recognition tasks involve writing the number of the correct picture on the line beside the corresponding vocabulary word. To assess sentence comprehension, students are asked to circle the letter of the sentence that best describes a given picture. The classification task consists of categorizing the names of three fruits and three vegetables that are labeled in a supermarket scene.

Administered in the multimedia lab at the International Studies Center, listening and speaking assessments include following directions and giving descriptions. For the directions activity, students listen to 10 statements and mark, color, or circle the corresponding images on a worksheet that displays 20 different images. For the descriptions activity, students describe orally a colorful classroom image.

Toward the end of the school year, Larchmont sixth graders spend one morning in assessment activities at the International Studies Center. The *Grade 6 Content-Based FLES Assessment* consists of six parts: one each for categorizing, reading, writing, and speaking, and two for listening. To categorize, students look at four different pictures, then select and copy from a list the four words that best describe each picture. The reading activity involves reading a short story carefully, then circling the best of three responses to each of four questions. For the writing activity, students write to Maria, a pen pal they have just met on the Internet. Their message must include two things about themselves, two things they enjoy doing, and a question for Maria to answer about herself. One listening activity involves looking at eight sets of four pictures, then choosing the one that best corresponds to a sentence that is spoken aloud twice. For the other listening activity, students look at a picture of a market and listen to and follow the directions given by an audiotape. The tape directs them to go shopping by placing a number on the items that they are told to buy. The speaking activity involves describing what they see in the market picture, including as many food items, people, numbers, colors, and other descriptive words as possible in two minutes. This activity is tape recorded.

Although students do not receive grades for their foreign language study, Lori Winne believes these assessments are important. "The test results will go to the students' foreign language teacher in junior high or high school, so they will know that these students don't have to start at square one," she says.

Program Evaluation

In 1994-95, the district's Evaluation Services Division conducted an assessment survey of the Toledo Public Schools elementary foreign language pilot program. The survey questionnaires were completed by 21 regular first through fourth grade teachers, two foreign language teachers, two principals, and parents. In general, the results indicated that the program had been well received and was recommended for continuation. All of the groups felt that the content-enriched approach was working very well and that it enhanced the regular curriculum.

Regular classroom teachers indicated that the regular curriculum was reinforced and enhanced by foreign language instruction. They noted that their students enjoyed the instruction and that they appeared to be learning the language. They considered the classroom activities to be varied and appropriate to the level of their students.

The two responding foreign language teachers indicated that the program was well designed and well implemented, and they agreed that the majority of the students were reaching the foreign language goals. They strongly supported the program philosophies and concepts and indicated that they had received strong support from the central administration, principals, and parents. One of the teachers felt that more resources were needed and that they needed more time for materials preparation and networking with other colleagues in the program.

The principals indicated that they felt the students were learning the foreign language and that they could see the continuity in the curriculum from grade to grade. One principal noted that the content-enriched approach was successful, that parents were pleased with the program, and that it should be expanded to more schools.

Parents were very pleased with the program, indicating that their children "talked about the foreign language at home and were enthusiastic about learning to communicate in a foreign tongue" (Toledo Public Schools, 1995, p. 2). Ninety-eight percent of the parents said they wanted their children to continue receiving foreign language instruction.

Challenges

Although the program in Toledo shows how much can be done with few resources, the funding limitations have an impact nonetheless. The schedule of two half-hour sessions per week is minimal. Much more could be accomplished with the addition of staff to teach additional classes. Students could achieve higher levels of proficiency with more hours of instruction per week.

Funding difficulties have also led to a major problem with articulation. Currently there is no foreign language in seventh grade in any of the junior high schools, and there is only one quarter of exploratory language (an introduction to three different languages) in the eighth grade. Establishing a foreign language program at the junior high level will require teachers and funding, as the three elementary foreign language teachers are already teaching full-time in their respective elementary schools.

Another challenge is how to strengthen parental support. Partly because of the small staff, the program's linkage with parents is minimal. There are no regular newsletter articles, parent support groups, or other indicators of parent involvement. Although parents interviewed stay in touch with the teacher through periodic phone calls, this is not a feasible communication approach for a program with over 200 students. Larchmont parents say they are supportive of the foreign language program, but have not become involved in ongoing, tangible ways. More involvement of parents could help leverage the school board for a stronger junior high language program to serve as a bridge for a well-articulated Grade 1–12 program.

Keys to Success

Principal Jeffrey Hanthorn says, "The number one essential feature of the program is a good teacher who really wants to do what she is doing." In Martínez, Larchmont certainly has such a teacher. Her combination of language skills, educational background, energy, and professionalism contribute immeasurably to the program's success. Her example demonstrates that an elementary school can implement a worthwhile, content-enriched foreign language program with just one teacher.

Second, the classes are enjoyable and motivating. One of the regular classroom teachers says that one of the main reasons for the program's success is "No grades!" Martínez's system of awarding points for language performance is a creative way to assess and motivate at the same time. The market system she uses helps her track the progress of the many students she sees each week, while it encourages students to participate without putting them under pressure.

Another factor that has contributed to the success of the program is content-enriched lessons. Hanthorn believes that the reinforcement that Larchmont students receive in their Spanish lessons has contributed to higher scores on standardized achievement tests in core subject areas. Regular classroom teachers have supported the program for similar reasons. They see the language lessons as strongly linked to the overall educational goals they are trying to achieve with their students.

One of the noteworthy characteristics of this program is that it is inclusive. Aside from a small number of students with multiple disabilities, every child in the school studies Spanish. This wide involvement in language learning contributes to the culture of the entire school as a source of pride for students, parents, and staff.

Finally, the key to long-term success for this program has been the ongoing commitment of staff at all levels within the school system. Important examples include Lori Winne's initial championing of the program, principal Jeffrey Hanthorn's contagious enthusiasm for it, María Martínez's innovative teaching, and the board of education's willingness to support the program when grant funding expired. The depth of support has been genuine and crucial to the program's continuation despite persistent fiscal challenges.

Richmond Elementary School

Portland Public Schools, Portland, Oregon

Borrowing an idea from Public Television's *Sesame Street*, Amy Grover has her 28 kindergarten students focus on a "letter of the day." As she writes on the board at the front of the room, Grover speaks slowly and clearly, and the children sitting around her on the carpet gradually learn to recognize the shape and sound of the day's letter. Grover helps them associate the letter with words they know, especially names of animals, leading to a song that features those animals, complete with hand gestures and sound effects. Most of the students have also learned the letters they need to read and write their own names. These are typical early literacy activities at the kindergarten level, but what makes them special in this instance is that for Amy Grover's students, the letters are not the familiar A, B, and C, but letters in the Japanese *hiragana* writing system. In the partial immersion Japanese language program at Richmond Elementary School in Portland, Oregon, there is attention to literacy skills development from the very beginning. By the fifth grade, students can read books and worksheets in Japanese and write their own geography reports in the language, in longhand or on a computer.

Program Overview
Richmond Elementary School's language program, which extends from kindergarten through fifth grade, is part of an articulated se-

quence that continues through high school. Initiated in 1989 in kindergarten, the Japanese language program began adding one grade each year, aiming to complete the sequence with a twelfth-grade program in the 2001-2002 school year. Since 1996, a tuition fee has been charged for the kindergarten program, but financial assistance is available if needed. The basic structure of the program involves teams of two teachers at each grade level, one offering instruction in English for half the day and the other teaching in Japanese for the other half. The two teachers plan together in order to integrate and reinforce content matter across the languages. As one program brochure says, "Through integrated thematic instruction, the teachers plan complementary lessons that reinforce the concepts that are part of the State of Oregon and Portland Public Schools' curriculum framework" (Portland Public Schools , 1997, p. 2). Subjects taught partly in Japanese include geography, health, art, science, literature,

8.01 ■

Program brochure

math, government, and history. The emphasis varies by grade level, but no subject is taught exclusively in English except English language arts.

Portland, the largest city in Oregon, has a population of about 510,000, and the school district is ethnically diverse. Sixty-seven percent of the district's students are Caucasian, 16% are Asian American, 10% are African American, 5% are Hispanic, and 2% are Native American. These proportions are mirrored as closely as possible by the 330 students participating in the Japanese language magnet program at Richmond Elementary School. Of the approximately 500 students attending the school, 24% qualify for free or reduced-cost lunches.

To apply for the program, parents of preschoolers fill out application forms in the spring preceding their entry into kindergarten. Because the program can accept only 56 new students per year, selection is by lottery. Applicants are categorized by gender, race, and geographic area of the city to ensure as close a reflection of city demographics as possible, though there are no quotas that must be met. Siblings of students already enrolled in the program have priority over other new applicants. There is also a mandatory meeting for the applying parents to discuss whether their child is well suited to the program. For the 1998-99 school year there were 22 siblings, leaving only 34 open spaces in the program. "There is always a waiting list," says Deanne Balzer, resource teacher.

Program Philosophy and Goals

The proposal to establish an elementary Japanese language program (Portland Public Schools, 1988) calls the program a "timely response to the increasing national awareness of the critical importance of linguistic resources to our economic and political interests, both at home and abroad" (p. 1). The proposal further notes that the program is an expression of the district's commitment to multicultural education and to meeting "varied academic needs and priorities" of the diverse student population. Citing authorities such as Helena

8.02 ■

JAPANESE MAGNET PROGRAM
Richmond Elementary School
2276 SE 41st
Portland, OR 97214
503 916-6220

JMP KINDERGARTEN GOALS

Kindergarten curriculum is often more exploratory than explanatory. Young learners are absorbing information and then trying to make sense of it.

We shall explore four main thematic units this year.****

1. THIS IS MY WORLD. (Health unit / Sept.-Oct.)
   Along with learning their numbers, colors, and basic Japanese vocabulary, we focus on a variety of health topics. Some of these are: my family and I, good health habits, self-concept activities, and dental health.

2. OFF WE GO! (Transportation Unit / Nov.-Dec.)
   Off we go! ... to Japan! In the Japanese classroom, we work towards a culminating activity of going to Japan! We hope to take a field trip to the airport during this unit. We will also learn about community helpers (e.g., policemen, fire fighters) and different modes of transportation.

3. SHOP TILL YOU DROP! (Economics Unit / Feb.-March)
   We focus on money concepts, the manufacturing process (raw materials to product) and the economic process (compensation for labor). Culminating activities include a working field trip to the bank where students "cash" their paycheck; a "shopping day" where students purchase products which they've made; and a bento picnic where students make their bento and invite parents for a picnic for Hanami (cherry blossom viewing).

4. CREEPY, CRAWLY, CRUNCHY CRITTERS!
   (Environment Unit / April-May)
   Our focus is on insects, but we also learn about other animals. We will discuss recycling and other environmental issues. In the English classroom we collect pop cans to adopt an acre of rain forest and an animal (such as a whale or a bat).

****Please be aware that not all topics will be covered in both classrooms.

JMP JAPANESE LANGUAGE GOALS

Japanese language skills have been divided into the
following areas:

LISTENING
- Tolerates not understanding every word but tries to
  attend to spoken Japanese: teachers, TV, books, tapes,
  records
- Can follow 1 to 2 step directions
- Follows teacher's instructions
- Begins to detect repeated language patterns

SPEAKING
- Progresses towards accurate pronunciation
- Sings various songs
- Begins to use words and patterned sentences with
  teachers and peers
- Begins to create phrases

READING
- Distinguishes Japanese characters
- Recognizes the *hiragana* in his/her name
- Recognizes a variety of simple words in *hiragana*

WRITING
- Can write first name in *hiragana* in correct stroke
  order
- Attempts to write other *hiragana* characters
- Attempts to copy simple words of one to two
  characters

Curtain (see Curtain & Pesola, 1994), the Japanese Immersion Planning Committee describe the advantages of an early start in foreign language learning and the benefits of a language immersion approach, noting that students in immersion programs "gain deeper insights into themselves and their own culture while learning the cultural patterns and values of the target language." The partial immersion model was chosen in part because of the difficulties posed by Japanese for native speakers of English and in part because partial immersion allows the school to serve native speakers of both English and Japanese.

The Japanese language program has six goals:

For students:
- To learn Japanese within the curriculum goals of Portland Public Schools.
- To learn Japanese language and culture.
- To develop a depth of understanding of the cultural/social skills and behaviors of Japan.

For teachers and administrators:
- To reach children from a variety of neighborhoods, cultures, socio-economic backgrounds, and ability levels.
- To produce students who are proficient in Japanese commensurate with the level of instruction provided.
- To present Japanese in a communication-rich environment and thereby draw on a child's natural language learning ability.

(Portland Public Schools, 1988, p. 4)

Within this framework, each grade has specific goals (see 8.02).

Program History

The Japanese program is the second partial immersion program in Portland. A Spanish program was begun in 1987, two years before Richmond's Japanese program started. Japanese was the logical choice for a second language program in the district. "Portland had a sister city relationship with Sapporo, Japan, for over 20 years," notes Deanne Balzer, resource teacher at Richmond Elementary School. "During the 1980s, there was a surge of Pacific Rim businesses and visitors in the Portland area." By 1987, a number of parents were actively advocating for a Japanese language program.

A planning committee began work in 1988, gathering information about immersion programs and about Japanese immersion programs in particular. To develop community support, a community advisory committee was established, which included members of the local Japanese business and education community. Other planning committee tasks included "developing student application and selection procedures, developing job descriptions for teachers and educational assistants, developing a transportation plan, preparing a curriculum outline, and recruiting and selecting teachers" (Leitner, 1990, p. 10). In addition, they tackled content issues such as how the three different Japanese alphabet systems should be treated, which sorts of Japanese customs should be included, and how math should be taught.

Despite the impressive accomplishments of the planning committee, a number of gaps remained when the program began in September 1989. "Because the program was new, it was difficult to anticipate student progress and to develop curriculum plans too far in advance," comments David Leitner (1990, p. 11) in his evaluation of the program after the first year. "While (the program's) teachers were able to follow the district curriculum in teaching different subject areas, the district does not have formal goals and objectives for teaching foreign languages . . . in immersion programs" (p.11). As a result, Deanne Balzer worked with the kindergarten team on developing curriculum, identifying appropriate materials, and planning lessons. The Japanese kindergarten teacher also learned from her English-speaking partner how to implement the district's kindergarten curriculum. As the program added one grade each year, Balzer and the teams of teachers for Grades 1 through 5 repeated the experience of establishing Japanese language goals and drafting and field-testing curriculum and materials.

In the Classroom

Students in the Japanese program have their day divided in half by language. If their morning is spent immersed in Japanese, the afternoon is in English, and vice versa. Each grade is handled by a two-teacher team, one teaching entirely in Japanese and the other teaching in English. Because there are two classes at each grade level, the teachers are able to alternate with the two groups. The subjects are not divided by language but are covered in shared thematic units in both Japanese and English.

Photo by Deanne Balzer

Photo by Atsuko Ando

Curriculum

No longer creating new curriculum goals each year, program staff have established a set of goals for Japanese learners at each grade level. The goals are divided into speaking, listening, reading, and writing skills and cultural themes. The curriculum for writing raised particularly difficult issues for the program planners, because Japanese uses several writing systems. In the end, it was decided to use only the three traditional systems through third grade to avoid confusion with English. The Romanized Japanese alphabet is introduced in fourth grade, where it is particularly useful in computer tasks. Writing skill goals for the first graders include the following:

- [Writes] first and last name with correct form and stroke order in both horizontal and vertical styles.
- Begins to write 46 *hiragana* variations and combinations.
- Attempts to write about 10 *kanji* (more difficult characters based on Chinese).
- Attempts to write common words.
- Writes the date and days of the week.
- Begins recording short phrases and sentences in a journal.

By fourth grade, these are the student writing goals:

- Uses *hiragana, katakana,* and *kanji* correctly in appropriate context.
- Writes 50 *kanji* with correct stroke order.
- Writes paragraphs and a short story.

(Portland Public Schools, 1998).

The program follows state curriculum guidelines for all subjects while meeting national foreign language standards. "There really aren't [district] standards for foreign languages," says former school board member Lucius Hicks. "The current [1998] Portland guidelines are a combination of seat time plus proficiency descriptions." This situation is undergoing a change as new guidelines are being developed for oral and literacy skills.

Since 1993, Portland State University has assisted in the drafting of specific Japanese language oral proficiency benchmarks for Grades 3 through 12. "The benchmarks are a bit of a challenge," Deanne Balzer says. "All students need to be at a certain place by a certain time." The process began with establishing standards for high school graduation and has been proceeding from those to standards for the lower grades. Assessment procedures are linked to the standards.

Because the program is content-based, the curriculum at each grade level is both a language and a content curriculum, the result of careful planning and annual revision by staff. Thus, when the state or district adopts new standards or textbooks for any elementary subject, Richmond's immersion curriculum has to be revised. According to Balzer, this has been a particular challenge in math, where new textbooks and standards emphasize problem-solving processes that ask students to analyze problems from multiple perspectives and explain reasons for answers. "The new math approaches are much more discussion- and literacy-oriented," Balzer says. These changes require not only teacher training time, but also planning time to decide which aspects are to be covered in which language. These changes may also necessitate new materials development efforts.

Visiting a Class

When a visitor enters Atsuko Ando's fifth-grade class during a geography lesson, the students stand in neat rows and bow. The large, sunny classroom is appealingly decorated with authentic materials from Japan as well as student work, including a great deal of writing in Japanese. Shelves display student-made paper-mâché globes, and there are two computers at the back of the room. About two dozen students, sitting at desks clustered in groups of four, are scanning Japanese reference books for information they can adapt to complete fact sheets about "nations" they have invented. When Ando rings a bell to call the class to attention, they quickly put their materials away, and one student comes forward from each cluster to pick up worksheets. Ando flips on the overhead projector and explains the directions, pointing at words and gesturing to clarify. She demonstrates how the answers are to be written and then has all students follow along to show that they have understood. On the reverse side of the worksheet are two paragraphs entirely in Japanese about geographical features. Before the students tackle the questions, Ando shows a transparency of the two paragraphs and the class reads them together. She asks for individuals to read specific sentences, pausing to ask questions and make clarifying comments, always in Japanese. Finally, the students turn back to the worksheet, trying to answer the written questions. The teacher circulates to help students having difficulties. The lesson ends a few minutes later when Ando identifies individuals to give their answers, and the rest of the class repeats. An onlooker more accustomed to American cultural norms has the impression of a very adult learning atmosphere in the classroom.

Classroom Activities

Students in the program progress dramatically from activities like the letter-of-the-day alphabet songs in kindergarten to the sophisticated geography reading and writing tasks in Atsuko Ando's fifth-grade class. Third grade is seen as the key year in that transition. "This is when the creative use of language starts," says Deanne Balzer. Homework is optional in first and second grades, she says, but that's no longer true by third. Special once-a-week classes in calligraphy are held in third grade. "It's hard to get all the students excited at once," says third-grade Japanese immersion teacher Joyce Iliff. "But I have noticed that most will follow if the teacher is excited and involved. Third graders like to know why they are doing things. If they understand why, then they are more into it."

Third-grade students not only consolidate literacy skills but also interact with a range of visitors from the community, such as an ice sculpture specialist, the Japanese author of a book about dinosaurs, recent Japanese immigrants, and Japanese people from the community who have been in America for more than 50 years. "The children cry when they hear about Japanese-Americans' experiences in camps during World War II," says Joyce Iliff. By third grade, students speak more Japanese in class. When students say anything in English that Iliff is certain they can say in Japanese, she insists on the translation. "There is a deeper buy-in at this level," Iliff says. "The children see that learning Japanese is not just about singing songs."

Another highlight of the third-grade class is cross-age tutoring in Japanese. When possible, high school students who are proficient in Japanese visit Richmond Elementary School to teach word processing and graphic design on computers with Japanese keyboards. Some of the high school students are especially interested in participating because Richmond has obtained software graphics programs through a federal grant. Between visits, the students communicate in Japanese by e-mail. Computers are also used by fifth-grade students who carry out research on the Internet in English, then write original summaries in Japanese.

Every spring, about 90% of the fifth graders in the program travel to Toyama, Japan, for two weeks, spending much of their time with Japanese families. Deanne Balzer and former Richmond principal Renee Ito-Staub assisted in establishing an English immersion program in a local private school there, so there are many opportunities for the Richmond students to form connections with Japanese peers. The purpose of the trip is primarily exploratory, to build cultural awareness. "It really motivates students to continue in the Japanese program into middle school, " Balzer says. Early in their sixth-grade year at Mount Tabor Middle School, the students write about their Japan experience, then visit Richmond Elementary to share their reports with fourth and fifth graders. Eighth graders also go on a two-week trip to Japan, but their experience is a bit more academic. They have tasks and research projects to accomplish.

Fundraising efforts offset much of the expense of the trips to Japan; the cost to families is approximately $500 per child, according to Balzer. There is scholarship support through the Japanese immersion parents organization, Oya No Kai, for those needing it. An annual auction is held to raise scholarship funds. The organization is currently investigating the possibility of a Japan trip for 11th-grade students as well.

Assessment

Since 1991, the immersion program has carried out annual videotaped oral interview assessments. Each kindergarten student brings a blank videotape to school at the end of the year and uses it to tape an interview with the teacher. The same tape is then used each year to add a new interview. "The interviews in kindergarten through second grade are short," says Deanne Balzer, "just a few minutes of answering simple questions." By third grade the interviews last 10 minutes, and fifth graders' interviews are usually 15 minutes long.

Beginning with third grade, the interviews follow Oregon Japanese Oral Proficiency Assessment procedures, which are being developed in conjunction with the state curriculum standards. The results have been encouraging. First developed to evaluate high school students of Japanese, the oral interviews were administered to fifth graders in the Japanese immersion program as an experiment. "The Richmond kids were beating high school students on the tests," Balzer says. The field-test versions of the procedures are being used for elementary-age learners. Although the state requires testing only at third and fifth grade during elementary school, students in the immersion program are assessed every year. "We want the children to become accustomed to the process, so that the official tests are no big deal," Balzer says.

Formal assessment of writing skills also begins in third grade, using tests developed by Richmond teachers working with Dr. Suwako Watanabe at Portland State University. To minimize the burden on immersion teachers, the tests are scored by Japanese language teaching assistants at the university. Both the written and oral assessments are linked to state standards, which in turn reflect national foreign language standards.

Complementing these formal tests are "work samples," which are examples of each student's work. The work sample system is not quite the same as a typical portfolio system, in which students might select the best examples of their own work. Mandated by the Oregon Department of Education, work samples are specified for content standards and benchmarks in each subject and for different grade levels. The work samples are "classroom assignments scored on a 1–6 point scale," and the scale is linked to "specific, consistent criteria" (Oregon Department of Education, 1998, p.2). Since standards have not been established for foreign language immersion programs, the Japanese program is using the state standards for English as a guide.

Articulation

Extra funding has enhanced articulation within the program. A grant from the Japanese Language Foundation, administered by the Japanese government, supported initial staffing costs at the middle-school level, providing much of the funds needed for teachers' salaries during the start-up phase.

As the immersion program has expanded, the need has increased for formal systems to ensure articulation, particularly between elementary and middle school and between middle school and high school. A Portland Public Schools Foundation grant for articulation has recently strengthened those systems. As a result of the grant-funded efforts, the Japanese program now has in place goals for elementary school, middle school, and high school, which include scope and sequence for Japanese language learning, *kanji* curriculum goals, and vocabulary specifications. Program staff have applied for funds to carry out Phase 2 of the articulation project, which would adjust student assessments to better reflect student achievement levels.

8.03

The Moshi Moshi Project

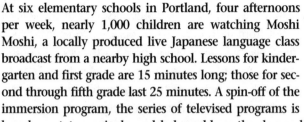

At six elementary schools in Portland, four afternoons per week, nearly 1,000 children are watching Moshi Moshi, a locally produced live Japanese language class broadcast from a nearby high school. Lessons for kindergarten and first grade are 15 minutes long; those for second through fifth grade last 25 minutes. A spin-off of the immersion program, the series of televised programs is based on state curricula and helps address the demand for Japanese language instruction that the magnet program cannot meet. Using skits, songs, and other high-interest activities, the programs begin preparing students to meet Oregon's second language standards. The non-Japanese-speaking classroom teachers who tune in the program may earn continuing education credits by attending staff development training every other week. In these sessions, they learn strategies, songs, activities, and cultural concepts for more effective teaching of Japanese. Japanese-speaking university students can earn academic credit by assisting the teachers in their classrooms during and after the Moshi Moshi broadcasts. "They help teachers extend some of the activities and integrate the Japanese lesson into the regular school day," says Moshi Moshi project director Mary Bastiani.

In addition to the live broadcasts, the Moshi Moshi project has produced four Japanese language videos based on topics from the interactive television program. Video topics include greetings, fruits and vegetables, animals, parts of the body, and numbers. Parents who purchase the videos use them and accompanying activity packets to help reinforce their children's Japanese language skills, particularly during the summer months. Two videos of songs are also available. Initially supported by grants from the U.S. Department of Education and the Omron Foundation, the Moshi Moshi project is also supported by over a dozen businesses and organizations. Since federal funding ended, ongoing support has come from county home-schooling funds.

"Moshi Moshi on Video" ordering information is available from Moshi Moshi Project, Portland Public Schools, 5210 N. Kerby, Portland, OR 97217 or bastiani@pps.k12.us. Telephone: (503) 916-3155. Up-to-date information about distance language learning in Portland Public Schools is available at the Web site: http://www.moshihola.org.

The People Behind the Program
Teachers

The pairs of English-speaking and Japanese-speaking teachers who share responsibility for two classes of 28 students at each grade level naturally learn a lot from each other. Their daily schedule includes a one-hour common planning time every morning to support coordination and sharing. The Japanese teachers may help their English-speaking partners with the points of Japanese culture and linguistic forms they are teaching, and the English-speaking teacher may need to familiarize the Japanese teacher with American educational norms and district and school policies and procedures. The successful teaming of a Japanese teacher with an English-speaking teacher is a combination of a good selection process and luck, according to Deanne Balzer. "It's a bit like an arranged marriage," she comments.

Japanese teacher Atsuko Ando acknowledges the importance of the partnership in her first year with the program. "I needed to learn about the American classroom and American discipline concepts like time out, consequences, and cool down," she says. "We had to spend a lot of time planning together at first," says Japanese teacher Joyce Iliff, who has been with the program for more than 7 years. "I've been teaching third grade with Mrs. Nelson for more than 6 years, though, so we spend much less time planning together now."

Barbara Garcia, an English-speaking teacher, has taught fourth and fifth grade in the Japanese program for more than 5 years and has over 30 years experience in elementary education. "We English teachers in the program at Richmond have a lot of responsibilities," she says, "especially compared to elementary school teachers in a regular program. We have twice the number of children, but the same expectations—about participation in meetings, spending time with kids, and administering standardized tests—as for teachers with half the number," Garcia says. "Initially we may also have to spend a lot of time training the Japanese teacher," she adds. Garcia says it took her 3 years to become comfortable with the materials, work load, and other aspects of the Japanese program.

Karen Damon, a first-grade English-speaking teacher, has over 25 years experience in elementary education. She also has seen a change in how she works with her Japanese partner. "It has always been a 50/50 partnership, but initially we planned week by week, and now it's more unit by unit. Quarterly we write report cards together." The two teachers function very closely as a team to ensure that the curriculum is covered and to address student behavior or parent issues, Damon says.

Spending half the day in a foreign language does not slow down children's development of skills in English, according to Richmond teachers. Comparing Richmond immersion students' English skills development to those of children in regular programs, Barbara Garcia says, "I see no real difference, but our students have many benefits, such as opportunities to speak in front of people, that others may lack." She notes that the Japanese program has access to funds through grants and from parent fund-raising activities that benefit the total program.

Both Garcia and Damon have stayed with the program despite the greater demands it makes of them, because they believe in its philosophy. "It's a team effort," says Damon. "The program wouldn't exist without support from administration, parents, and all the teachers." She says that the program acknowledges the views and feelings of everyone involved. "We listen to the kids and allow them to develop a voice. Parents are important also; we're informing them or listening to them all the time." Garcia agrees about the Japanese program's teamwork philosophy and its success. "The program builds flexibility, security, and self-esteem," she adds.

Board of Education, Principal, and Resource Teacher

"The board has been extremely supportive of the Japanese magnet program," board member Lucius Hicks says. "It was 3 or 4 years ago," he recalls, "when we had to develop the middle school pathway, and we had to come to grips with this program as a commitment and not just an experiment." When financial problems threatened the program, Hicks says the board's stance was, "What do we need to focus on to meet the mission?" His own vision for the program includes more sustainable funding and a more systematic approach to support for parents, such as access to Japanese language learning and daily electronic updates on program activities or even homework assignments. Hicks would like to see more immersion programs like the Japanese one. "The program should be a kind of beta test," says Hicks. "We should be expanding immersion offerings, borrowing ideas from Richmond Elementary on how to do it."

Renee Ito-Staub, recently retired principal of Richmond Elementary School, was not only instrumental in convincing the city government to support the Japanese program, but she also served on the planning committee that established it. Together, Ito-Staub and Deanne Balzer set a standard of a high level of commitment to the program. In collaboration with committees and work groups, the current principal and Balzer ensure that the program runs smoothly, address the thorny areas of curriculum and assessment, and explore new directions.

Deanne Balzer, whose parents were missionaries, grew up in Japan and speaks the language fluently. Her position is only part-time, but it's an important one. In addition to her involvement in assessment and curriculum projects, Balzer oversees the student intern program and serves as the program's institutional memory. "Deanne's position is key," says Mary Bastiani, formerly the district's foreign language curriculum coordinator. "She pulls all the pieces together." Ito-Staub's successor, Rebecca McWaters, has continued the close partnership with Balzer in all matters regarding the immersion program.

Parents

"Learning a second language is important for every child," says Marsha Brecheen, whose daughter is in first grade at Richmond. "It's almost arrogant not to learn another language—children in every other independent nation do." Juanita Lewis, mother of a fifth grader in the program, agrees about the benefits of second language learning. "There will always be adversity (in life), but my daughter will be better prepared," Lewis says. "Knowing Japanese will open doors for her." Lewis is particularly pleased with the racial variety at the school. "I'm very, very pleased with Richmond," she says. "Race is not an issue here, so my daughter won't be internalizing racism." Lewis expects that her daughter "will be open to more than just the neighborhood, Portland, or America" as a result of participating in the Japanese program.

Both Lewis and Brecheen say their children find ways to use Japanese outside school. "My daughter has given her puppy a Japanese name and speaks to it in Japanese," Brecheen says. Lewis says that her daughter translates at stores, counts in Japanese, and uses the language in music and games. "She doesn't like fake opportunities to speak, but genuine ones–yes." Lewis describes Richmond's array of extracurricular language-related opportunities as "a banquet" because there is so much to choose from.

Both mothers are impressed with the teachers in the program at Richmond and with the partnership the teachers forge with parents. Brecheen describes the teachers as "accessible," and Lewis says, "If there's an issue we just talk." They also appreciate the newsletters that they receive regularly. "Parents are very much a part of the school," says Lewis. Both she and Brecheen have been active participants in the program, Brecheen helping in the classroom as a docent, and Lewis serving on the board of the parent support group. "Those meetings start at seven and sometimes go on until ten," she says.

"I was worried about my daughter last year because she left kindergarten without seeming to be able to read," says Brecheen. "But now (toward the end of first grade), she is reading like crazy. I had no idea she could read so well in Japanese; at this point her English reading skills are just catching up." Deanne Balzer emphasizes the important role parents can play in the early elementary years. "First language skills do impact the Japanese side," she says. "We encourage all parents to work with their children on English literacy skills at home."

8.04 ∎

Guidance for Parents Considering a Japanese Program

Parents who are considering a Japanese language program for a child are encouraged to explore the idea with the child before applying. Richmond Elementary has developed a two-page illustrated guide to help. The first five items in the guide are statements accompanied by pictures. Photocopied excerpts from illustrated Japanese storybooks are labeled, "I would like to be able to read these books." The statement, "I would like to learn how to write like this," appears above a photo of a Richmond student writing *hiragana* script with a brush. These are other illustrated items on the discussion guide sheet:

- I would like to know more about the people who wear this kind of clothing.
- I would be willing to try this food.
- I would like to visit a place like this.

The illustrated items are followed by statements for parents to discuss with their child:

- I would like to speak another language.
- I solve problems with other kids without hitting.
- I like to try new things.
- I am comfortable about changing activities often during the day.
- Talk about how your child would deal with something that is hard or frustrating. What would he or she do?

Finally, the guide suggests activities for parents to do with their child, observing the child's reaction, interest, or involvement. Activities include hosting a Japanese guest, visiting a Japanese market, and looking over books about Japan at a public library.

Oya No Kai

Parent involvement was mentioned in the 1988 proposal to establish the Japanese partial immersion program. Parents, the proposal stated, would be invited to join committees, accompany field trips, encourage students to read at home, and

Photo by Kristen Quevedo

make costumes and decorations for plays and festivals. Parents may also "raise funds for school projects," the program planners suggested (Portland Public Schools, 1988, p. 12).

Once the program began, however, parent involvement far exceeded these modest expectations. During the first year, 31 parents donated approximately 700 hours to program-related activities. They also formed a group on their own initiative, calling it *Oya No Kai,* which translates as "parent association." The purpose of the association was "to support program activities as well as to support parents of program students"(Leitner, 1990, p. 17). During the first year, the group met three times and established committees to support communication, social and cultural activities, and a summer program for children. Oya No Kai has continued to expand, providing volunteer and financial support for the entire magnet program from kindergarten through twelfth grade. In the 1996-97 school year, Oya No Kai was able to contribute nearly $19,000 to the Japanese program. They paid for Japanese books and supplies, field trips, and receptions for Japanese visitors. The group issues a monthly newsletter, *JMP Oshirase,* during the school year informing teachers, parents, and others in the community about past and future events such as fundraising activities, PTA meetings, and class projects. This parent organization has made possible a weekly Japanese calligraphy class for third graders, purchased bilingual dictionaries for the school library, and provided funds for fourth and fifth graders to visit a soy sauce factory and for third graders to smell the roses at authentic Japanese gardens. In 1997, Oya No Kai was granted legal status as a non-profit organization with the ability to receive tax-deductible donations.

8.05 ▪

JMP OSHIRASE

Japanese Magnet Program Newsletter for Richmond Elementary, Mt. Tabor Middle and Grant High School · Jan. 2000

Join Our Interns for an Evening

On Thursday, January 20, Oya No Kai, Inc. will be holding its next General Meeting in the Mt Tabor Cafetorium starting at 7:00 pm. The Board of Directors of Oya No Kai, Inc. cordially invites everyone to attend what should be an enjoyable and fun-filled adult evening. The JMP Interns have planned an exciting, hands on evening demonstrating many of their cultural skills and heritage. You will have an opportunity to participate in a Tea Ceremony, practice your Calligraphy, learn the proper way to dress in a Kimono, and even how to prepare Onigiri (Rice Balls). The JMP is lucky to have such talented interns who are eager to share their skills with our parent group. This is a great way to meet all of the JMP interns who work with your children every day at school.

Childcare will be provided. Children are asked not to

participate in this evenings demonstrations. Please take this chance to get to know the interns and then invite them to your home. They would enjoy sharing these skills with you and children on a one-to-one basis.

8.06

Summer Camp Programs

Kurabu, a Japanese counterpart to "El Club," Portland's Spanish immersion summer camp program, was created by parents "to allow their children to continue actively learning Japanese in an informal, fun setting, and stay in touch with their Richmond School buddies over the summer" (*JMP Oshirase*, January/February 1998, p. 1). Kurabu provides elementary students with two weeks of field trips, sports, cooking, games, and art activities as a means to learn Japanese. The program is open to Japanese and non-Japanese children in first through fourth grades who have some Japanese language skills, whether or not they are enrolled in the Richmond Elementary School Japanese program. The tuition fee is about $200. As the parent newsletter says, Kurabu "provides the opportunity for our children to be in a group with Japanese children who are living in Portland, or those who have learned Japanese in their families" (*JMP Oshirase*, January/February 1998, p. 1). Each group of 20 campers is supervised by two adult bilingual counselors, and the program director is qualified and experienced in Japanese culture, language immersion education, and recreation. Parents provide volunteer support, and the city parks program provides the institutional infrastructure. At the end of the program each summer, Kurabu joins forces with its Spanish sister program, El Club, to stage an international festival with colorful booths that the children have built and filled with crafts and food.

Oya No Kai has recently helped establish a second Japanese immersion camp, Shizen Kyampu ("nature camp"), for children in fourth through eighth grades. A weeK–long sleep away camp, Shizen Kyampu participants come from Sapporo and a number of sites in Oregon. The 50 campers spend the week focusing on science-related activities, all in Japanese.

Summer Camp Programs

In addition to raising money and contributing funds for program supplies and activities, Oya No Kai parents devote many hours inside and outside the school to support the program. They act as cultural resources in the classroom, volunteer for school cafeteria and playground responsibilities, host visiting Japanese college students in their homes, and locate additional hosts in the community if necessary. Oya No Kai takes the initiative to bring Japanese immersion parents together, urging them "to meet parents from other classes—we are all in this together" (*JMP Oshirase*, 1997, p. 2). Up-to-date information about Oya No Kai is available on the organization's website at http://www.oyanokai.org.

In 1994, Oya No Kai alumni and civic leaders established the Japanese Immersion Foundation, which has a broader focus than the parent association. The foundation works to strengthen immersion program linkages with Japanese civic organizations and fosters cooperation and communication among Japanese immersion programs in Oregon and throughout the United States.

Teacher Aides

Each year, the Japanese Language Exchange program, known as J-LEX, sends about 50 teachers or teachers in training to the United States to serve as assistant teachers. The program is overseen by the Japanese Ministry for Foreign Affairs. Selected for their English skills, about a dozen teachers are placed in Oregon, and Richmond Elementary usually can count on one or two annually.

In addition, about nine Japanese student interns assist classroom teachers. These interns are sponsored by several Japanese organizations, notably the New Global Peace Language Institute, which supports the teaching of Japanese. Besides assisting in the Moshi Moshi project at Richmond, the interns serve as teacher aides in each of the immersion classes. They help with small-group work, tutoring, and other individualized instruction, and serve as cultural resources.

Students

Greg Chaffin and Olivia Weick, fifth graders in the Japanese program, are enthusiastic about learning Japanese. Olivia's favorite classroom activity is keeping a journal, but Greg prefers geography: "learning about other countries and making up our own." He also enjoys learning the *kanji* script. Both students practice the language at home: Olivia by reading and Greg by speaking with his brother, who is in the sixth-grade program at Tabor Middle School. Olivia says that she likes to speak the language and will probably do fine in Japan, "But I'm embarrassed about speaking it when my parents push it." They say Japanese language study is fun and challenging, "and it's an advantage, like being smarter, if you speak two languages," Olivia says. "I think it's easier to learn a language when you're young." Both students are looking forward to the two-week trip to Japan. "I'm going to stay two extra weeks," Greg says. "I'll be staying with Japanese friends who came and stayed at our house."

Program Funding and Administration

Despite magnet funding, the Japanese language program has experienced more than its share of financial challenges. One budget cut led to the loss of paid classroom aides, who have been replaced with parent volunteers and student interns. More than in most other programs, there is a reliance on local donations and the parent support group, even for some staff salaries. Funds provided by student tuition cover the salary of the English-speaking kindergarten teacher, for example, allowing the program to operate a full-day kindergarten.

The school has also been successful at attracting a number of grants from a variety of sources. The Richmond principal and a grant-seeking team made up of parents and one teacher explore funding possibilities and needs. In addition to covering the first 3 years' costs of the Moshi Moshi project, grants have supported staff development activities, test development, and the hiring of substitute teachers. Grants also pay for guests to teach special Japanese language and culture lessons, such as those on ice sculpture and music.

The team approach to finding grants is typical of the collaborative leadership style at Richmond Elementary, where teams and work committees address a large range of school and program areas. In addition to the parent and grants committees, there is a site council made up of teachers, a magnet program parent, a neighborhood parent, and other school staff. This council considers such issues as student achievement, summer school offerings, and activities to support parents. A "magnet team" of Japanese teachers meets once a month to discuss articulation, curriculum development, and discipline. Other committees involve parents, school administrators, and teachers in joint decision making on school goals, technology initiatives, and curriculum.

Challenges

Two challenges that the Japanese program faces are tight finances and the potential for teacher burnout. Funding issues have been a challenge to this successful language program almost since it began. By the second year of operation, an ambitious plan for annual program evaluation had to be dropped because of lack of funds. Only one program evaluation has been carried out. Another casualty of fiscal problems was the immersion coordinator. The position was dissolved in 1994 and not resumed until 1999, particularly imperiling articulation efforts as the program grew. In recent years, budget cuts have forced the program to eliminate the paid classroom aides. Like other parents and a number of district administrators, Marsha Brecheen is concerned about the fiscal problems the program is facing because of shrinking tax support for the public schools in Portland. "I just have an uneasy feeling about it," Brecheen says. "Property tax limitations and the lack of a sales tax have hit Portland schools hard."

Although the teachers at Richmond Elementary School are exceptionally dedicated, their work load can be overwhelming. Average class size in other district elementary schools is only 20, but in Richmond's program the classes have 28 children. Teacher pay is adjusted for the increased number of students. Still, each teacher in the program sees over 50 children each day, with a correspondingly large burden of assessment responsibilities and parent meetings. For English teachers working with new Japanese teachers, the amount of work has been particularly daunting, because they are responsible for many aspects of the training and orientation of their Japanese colleagues. English teachers tend to stay with the program for only two or three years, according to Renee Ito-Staub, but Japanese teachers stay longer.

Keys to Success

Parent involvement is a notable key to Richmond's success. A visitor seeking even a brief introduction to the Japanese language program will immediately be impressed by the dedication and accomplishments of the parents. Parents of immersion students have taken an unusual leadership role in supporting communication within the program, maintaining staff positions, and raising funds that go far beyond an annual auction or cultural fair.

The second key to the success of the program has been the creative ways that the school staff, district administrators, and parents have found to respond to financial difficulties. The use of Japanese student interns to help off-set the loss of paid teaching aides has been largely successful. Alternative funding sources have ranged from the National Endowment for the Humanities and the government of Japan to the local university and area businesses. In the case of the Japanese language magnet program at Richmond Elementary, the expression "community buy-in" is meant in a literal as well as a figurative sense.

Perhaps the most important key to the success of the program is the combination of leadership and effective team work. Renee Ito-Staub brought a spirit of innovation to the task of beginning the program, and her collaborative style helped the program gain enthusiasm and support from others, as they came together for a range of tasks. The partnerships that resource teacher Deanne Balzer has forged with the current principal, the teachers in the program, and others have continued to strengthen the program despite fiscal challenges. Teaching teams provide built-in alignment among classes and promote professional development through peer sharing. Other teams and work groups pursue funding possibilities, revise curricula, and develop assessment procedures. It is the feeling of team spirit at Richmond Elementary that has also led to a positive relationship between magnet program students and others at the school and in the neighborhood.

The success of the program has not been adequately documented through formal program evaluations, but other evidence is easy to find. In 1994, Richmond was named a model program by the Center for Applied Japanese Language Studies. During the 1994-95 school year, Richmond served as a mentor program to a private Japanese language school that was in its first year of operation. There continues to be a long waiting list of parents wishing to enroll their children in the Richmond program, and there is almost no attrition in student numbers between kindergarten and fifth grade. In addition, Richmond students continue to perform well on district-wide tests. When funds do permit another thorough program evaluation, there is little doubt that the results will be overwhelmingly positive.

Conclusion

These seven model programs represent a range of strategies and accomplishments. Together, they also provide insight into the strengths of early foreign language programs and the challenges they face. It is, therefore, instructive to look at 10 critical program elements and identify best practices and areas requiring further attention.

1. Implementing National Standards

All seven of the model programs profiled here are implementing the five Cs of the national foreign language standards. In each instance, the local district or school has found effective ways to incorporate national standards while following local or state guidelines, not only for language instruction, but often for content areas as well. In some districts, such as Springfield, the five Cs explicitly form a core element of the curricula for all grades. In other cases, such as Prince George's County and Ephesus Road Elementary School, the content-related curricula address the standards in an integrated, almost organic way. It is interesting to note that none of the programs has adopted textbooks to form the core of its instructional program. Rather, materials are identified or developed that connect language learning to the immediate context or to specific lessons in the regular curriculum.

2. A Focus on Content

Although there was no intention in the project design to single out programs with content-based or content-enriched curricula, all seven of the model programs selected use one or the other. The language curricula in the seven model programs include topics from math and science to history and geography—virtually every subject, including English language arts. Several of the regular classroom teachers mention that foreign language study contibutes to students' English vocabulary building and to their reading and writing skills.

How the content-related language curricula are devised, implemented, and revised depends to some extent on program size and type. The seven model programs vary in how systematically they incorporate regular course content in language instruction. Those with the most formally established curricula are the district-wide programs, such as those in Springfield and Glastonbury, and the immersion programs, such as those in Portland and Prince George's County. In these programs, language curricula are aligned with curricula in the subject areas at the district level, and they are revised as the district curricula are revised. At Bay Point Elementary in Florida, on the other hand, although the language class content is closely tied to the content of regular classes, curriculum development and revision can be handled less formally, because only one school is involved.

3. Articulation and Alignment

Language instruction in the elementary grades frequently emphasizes activities that are creative and involve oral communication, with less attention to accuracy or written forms. As a result, there can be a disconnect when students move to the higher grades, where there is more emphasis on textbooks, grammar, and formal assessment. The challenge is compounded in decentralized districts, in which a school-based management approach may favor institutional autonomy at the expense of articulation with programs in other schools. Where language programs are offered in several schools in the district, it can be difficult to coordinate the instructional pace and content. The model programs profiled here have addressed these challenges through meetings, teaching exchanges, and standardization of curricula and assessment.

Meetings are one of the keys to effective articulation. In Springfield, for example, there are meetings of foreign language teachers in the elementary grades, voluntary monthly meetings of all foreign language teachers, and workshops that bring together all the foreign language teachers and school principals in the district.

Standardizing curriculum goals across schools has been an important means of supporting articulation and alignment in several of the programs. In Glastonbury, articulation is ensured through through this means as well as through coordination of assessment activities and an innovative program of exchange teaching. From time to time, the foreign language teachers trade classes: Elementary school teachers move to a high school and vice versa. If the teachers cannot exchange teaching responsibilities, observations of other teachers' classes are arranged instead.

To ensure alignment among elementary programs as well as articulation with middle schools, schools in Chapel Hill have collaboratively developed exit outcomes and a system-wide test for foreign language students at the end of the fifth grade.

4. Teaching Methods

Learning a language is a lot of fun, according to students in these model programs. Teachers keep their students motivated through age-appropriate, enjoyable lesson activities, many involving pair- or small-group work. In the elementary grades, songs are popular, especially ones fitting new lyrics to familiar tunes. Teachers at Ephesus Road Elementary School and Bay Point Elementary School have devised particularly creative guessing games and simulations that educate, entertain, and motivate learners and bring together students from different grade levels. Teachers in the middle-school grades have introduced an element of theater to their classes also, as exemplified in the lessons observed in the French immersion classes in Prince George's County. Most activities in the classes observed had a strong focus on communication and student interaction and a minimum of the tedious "listen and repeat" kind of instruction.

5. Technology

These programs have made a number of strides in the use of technology, but one expects greater things to come as schools become better equipped and teachers become more skilled. Training staff in the effective use of computer-based resources is a major focus of in-service staff development in nearly every model program. Several of the districts are also increasing younger learners' access to computers. The program at Ephesus Road Elementary is notable in its use of interactive Web-based communication with other French language programs around the world, and students in Portland are making increasing use of e-mail and other computer features. In Portland and in Glastonbury, distance learning technology is enabling increasing numbers of students to become learners of less commonly taught languages.

6. Program Evaluation

Program evaluation is not a widely shared strong point among the model programs. In several cases, there has been a single program evaluation effort, sometimes carried out with a nearby university or another outside institution. The program in Portland, for example, was initiated with a plan for regular program evaluation, but this was discontinued after only one year because of budget difficulties.

Notable among the model programs in this area is Glastonbury, which conducts a thorough program evaluation every 5 years. District staff survey staff, parents, and former students; administer tests; review state and national standards; and look closely at specific program areas, such as curriculum and use of technology.

7. Student Assessment

At least four assessment practices merit attention. First is the Home Assessment System at Bay Point Elementary School in Pinellas County, Florida, in which students take home task cards that parents sign, indicating that they have seen their child perform the language activity. This system involves parents, regular classroom teachers, and FLES teachers in the students' language learning process, lets students proceed at their own pace, and provides a portfolio of students' foreign language performance to be passed on as the students move from one level to the next.

María Martínez at Larchmont Elementary School in Toledo assesses students' oral proficiency and participation by awarding *puntos* (points) that are exchanged for imitation pesos to be used to purchase food, arts, and crafts at the end-of-year *mercado* (market). By adding up each student's points, Martínez can get a good idea of how much they participate and how proficient they are.

A third example of sound assessment is in Springfield, where classroom progress indicators and assessment activities are suggested for grade-level outcomes specified in the district-wide curriculum. The curriculum is organized according to the five Cs of the national standards, and assessment activities include learning logs, teacher checklists, and role plays.

Finally, the Japanese Magnet Program in Portland is implementing several innovative assessment strategies, notably in the use of videotaped interviews. Beginning in kindergarten, students are videotaped in dialogue with a teacher. Interviews reflect curriculum goals, which are based on standards set by the district and state. The program has also begun using "work samples," a variation of portfolio assessment that incorporates an evaluative dimension that is often lacking in this popular approach. The work samples are linked to state-mandated content standards and are assessed on a standardized six-point scale.

8. Funding

Typically, these model programs have received grant funds from state or federal sources, particularly during the start-up phase. The pre-implementation and early implementation years of foreign language programs require the greatest concentration of resources. Curricula and evaluation procedures need to be developed, books and other instructional materials must be purchased, teachers need to be found and trained, and there may be a need for extra supervisory or support personnel as well. Most programs are able to diversify and localize their funding as they mature, relying on federal and state grants for special needs such as program evaluation, articulation with post-secondary programs, or expanded uses of technology. The programs in Glastonbury and Portland have pursued particularly creative approaches to funding.

9. Professional Development

Professional development is critical during the early stages of a foreign language program, and it continues to be important as the programs mature, curricula change, and new technology is introduced. The programs in Toledo and Prince George's County have addressed these needs in creative ways. The foreign language program in Toledo has offered a low-cost summer language camp in which teachers can try out new skills, and the program in Maryland has offered university courses to teachers. In many of the model programs, foreign language teachers regularly attend professional conferences, such as the national conference of the American Council on the Teaching of Foreign Languages, and often present sessions or lead workshops. Staff in model programs also participate in in-service teacher training workshops organized at the district level, such as the monthly magnet curriculum trainings offered in Pinellas County and the workshops organized by Kathleen Riordan in Springfield. The "pre-start-up" activities in Chapel Hill are also worth noting. Foreign language teacher Carol Orringer visited elementary schools around the Chapel Hill district, teaching demonstration lessons that won the hearts and minds of skeptical regular classroom teachers. In Glastonbury, staff development efforts have been enhanced through grant funding from the Defense Education Act.

10. Advocacy

In nearly all of the model programs, outreach to the community, visibility at the school and district levels, and involvement of parents have been important to initiating programs, expanding them, or keeping them going during times of tight budgets. In most cases, advocacy for the programs involves media attention. From Toledo to

Portland, all have been featured on local television stations. Newspaper articles appear in *The Washington Post* about the students in the French immersion program in Prince George's County, and *The Chapel Hill News* has often featured stories about the French classes at Ephesus Road Elementary School.

Political connections have been important to programs as different as the one in Springfield, where the superintendent is a major advocate for early foreign language education, and the one at Ephesus Road Elementary, where the two foreign language teachers have served on the school governance committee for several years. Regular program newsletters, foreign language fairs, and shows are among other ways that program staff have captured and kept popular support. Finally, the tireless efforts of individual program representatives, such as those mentioned in each of the program descriptions, have made an enormous difference: As Kathleen Riordan says, "One can never attend too many meetings."

The Future: Changes and Challenges

Foreign language programs for younger learners are undergoing rapid change in two key areas. Perhaps the most evident is in the use of technology. More programs now have their own Web sites than when this project began in the late 1990s. The computer-assisted elements associated with distance learning are more widely accessible than ever, and an increasing number of classrooms are being equipped to take advantage of these resources. Already, foreign language students at Ephesus Road Elementary in North Carolina are exchanging e-mail messages with other students of French in Morocco, Guyana, Korea, and 10 other countries.

Curriculum is the other area where rapid changes are taking place, reflecting the impact of the national standards for foreign language learning. As national standards are being adopted and adapted at the state and district levels in all subject areas, foreign language programs have had to revise their curricula to keep pace. As Deanne Balzer in Portland notes, when there is a dramatic change in teaching approaches in any content area, content-based and content-enriched language programs have to adjust.

Two areas stand out as requiring further attention in the coming years: student assessment and program evaluation. If schools are to find support for initiating foreign language programs and retaining funding for them, they must be able to demonstrate how well students are progressing and how effective the programs are. At present, few foreign language programs assess the language achievements and skills of learners in a systematic way. The work of programs in Portland and Glastonbury may be particularly important as this issue receives more attention in the future. Assessment approaches that go beyond or supplement non-evaluative portfolios are needed. In response to an emphasis on accountability and tied to securing and retaining funding, language program evaluation will also need to be carried out more rigorously and systematically in the future.

It may be that the areas experiencing the most change, curriculum and technology, will become important tools in addressing the areas most needing improvement, student assessment and program evaluation. As mentioned, foreign language curricula are changing to reflect national standards of language learning. Because the national standards require programs to specify language course content and student outcomes in systematic ways, assessment activities can address these goals, as is done in the language program in Portland. The standards provide part of the framework necessary for developing systems for evaluating students' language learning and assessing program effectiveness.

Technology is also contributing to improved assessment. CD-ROMs and the Internet, combined with audio- and video-recording technology, are helping to solve some of the logistical difficulties involved in carrying out assessment. Programs in Toledo and Portland have begun exploring some of the potential benefits in this area.

One certainty is that in the coming years, foreign language education for younger learners will continue to develop and improve, reflecting national priorities, local commitment, and the contributions to excellence as exemplified in such programs as the seven featured in this book.

References

American Council on the Teaching of Foreign Languages. (1989). *ACTFL proficiency guidelines.* Yonkers, NY: Author.

Brown, C. (1995a). The case for foreign languages: The Glastonbury program. *Perspective, 7(2).*

Brown, C. (1995b). *Foreign language curriculum review: Executive summary.* Glastonbury, CT: Glastonbury Public Schools.

Brown, C. (1998). The people factor in the Glastonbury Public Schools. In G.C. Lipton (Ed.), *A celebration of FLES** (pp. 7–12). Chicago: National Textbook Co.

Center for Applied Linguistics. (1997). *Formative evaluation study of the French immersion magnet program, Prince George's County Public Schools.* Washington, DC: Author.

Connecticut State Board of Education. (1987). *1986–87 Connecticut assessment of educational progress in foreign language.* Hartford, CT: Author.

Curtain, H., & Pesola, C.A. (1994). *Languages and children: Making the match: Foreign language instruction for an early start, grades K–8* (2nd ed.). White Plains, NY: Longman.

Glastonbury Public Schools. (1999a). *FLES curriculum 2–5, grades 2–4, revised 9/19/97, grade 5 to be revised.* Glastonbury, CT: Author.

Glastonbury Public Schools. (1999b). *Spanish curriculum.* Unpublished draft.

Harris, J.L. (1998). *Report on the Chapel Hill–Carrboro City Schools K–12 World Language Program.* Unpublished draft.

Heining-Boynton, A. (1990). The development and testing of the FLES Program Evaluation Inventory. *Modern Language Journal, 74*(4), 432–439.

Jicha, H. (1997, Spring). The French corner. *The Ephesus Roadrunner.* Chapel Hill, NC: Ephesus Road Elementary School.

JMP Oshirase (November 1997).

JMP Oshirase (January/February 1998).

Kiebish, J. (1999). Keynote speech at the Glastonbury NNELL Advocacy, Articulation, and Curriculum Development Conference, Hartford, CT.

Krashen, S., & Terrell, T. (1983). *The natural approach: Language acquisition in the classroom.* Oxford: Pergamon Press.

Leitner, D. (1990). *Japanese Language Magnet Program, 1989–90 evaluation report.* Portland, OR: Portland Public Schools, Department of Research and Evaluation.

Loeb, M. (1999). *Directory of two-way bilingual immersion programs in the U.S., 1998–99 supplement.* Washington, DC, and Santa Cruz, CA: Center for Research on Education, Diversity & Excellence.

Massachusetts Department of Education (1999). *Massachusetts foreign languages curriculum framework.* Boston, MA: Author. (Available from the Massachusetts Department of Education, 350 Main Street, Malden, MA 02148)

Met, M. (Ed.). (1998). *Critical issues in early second language learning.* New York, NY: Scott-Foresman/Addison Wesley.

Nakamura, D. (1999, May 19). Bilingual honors for bilingual students. *The Washington Post,* p. B3.

National Standards in Foreign Language Education Project. (1996). *Standards for foreign language learning: Preparing for the 21st century.* Yonkers, NY: Author.

North Carolina Department of Public Instruction. (1999) *Second languages: Standard course of study and grade level competencies, K–12, draft 9/99.* Raleigh, NC: Author.

Ohio Department of Education. (1996) *Foreign languages: Ohio's model competency-based program.* Columbus, OH: Author.

Oregon Department of Education. (1998). *Oregon standards.* Portland, OR: Author.

Pinellas County Public Schools. (n.d.). *Expectations K–5, foreign language.*

Pinellas County Schools. (1998). *Chispas: A curriculum guide for the Pinellas County FLEX program.* St. Petersburg, FL: Author.

Portland Public Schools. (1988). *Proposal for establishing an elementary Japanese language magnet program at Richmond Elementary School beginning in fall 1989.* Portland, OR: Author.

Portland Public Schools. (1997). *Learning together: Japanese language elementary magnet program at Richmond School.* Portland, OR: Author.

Portland Public Schools. (1998). *Japanese Magnet Program (JMP) curriculum overview for kindergarten through grade five, 1998–1999.* Portland, OR: Author.

Prince George's County Public Schools. (1998a). *1997–1998 foreign language enrollment study, grades 7–12.* Upper Marlboro, MD: Author.

Prince George's County Public Schools. (1998b). *The French immersion program in the middle school curriculum guide.* Upper Marlboro, MD: Author.

Rhodes, N.C., & Branaman, L.E. (1999). *Foreign language instruction in the United States: A national survey of elementary and secondary schools.* McHenry, IL, and Washington, DC: Delta Systems and the Center for Applied Linguistics.

Riordan, K. (1998). The Springfield story. In M. Met (Ed.), *Critical issues in early second language learning* (pp. 262–266). New York, NY: Scott-Foresman/Addison Wesley.

Scholastic News en Español, April 1998, Edition 1, Vol. 54, No. 7.

Sheppard, K. (1994). *Content–ESL across the USA: Volume I. A technical report* (Report submitted to the Office of Bilingual Education and Minority Languages Affairs, U.S. Department of Education). Washington, DC: Center for Applied Linguistics.

Shuler, M. (1997, January). Second grade—Mexico unit lesson plan. *Glastonbury Language Department GOALS 2000 Grant News, 1*(1), 6–7.

Springfield Public Schools. (1996). *World language learning outcomes, 1996–1997 working draft.* Springfield, MA: Author.

Springfield Public Schools. (1998). *World language learning outcomes, grades K–5, working document.* Springfield, MA: Author.

State of Florida, Department of Education. (1996). *Florida curriculum framework, preK–12 Sunshine State standards and instructional practices, foreign languages.* Tallahassee, FL: Author.

Thompson, L. (1997). *Foreign language assessment in grades K–8: An annotated bibliography of assessment instruments.* McHenry, IL, and Washington, DC: Delta Systems and Center for Applied Linguistics.

Toledo Public Schools, Evaluation Services. (1995). *Elementary foreign language pilot program 1994/1995 survey assessment results.* Toledo, OH: Author.

Toledo Public Schools. (1997). *Toledo Public Schools content-based elementary foreign language program.* Toledo, OH: Author.

Tyson, T. (1997, February 9). Ephesus students celebrate 100th day. *The Chapel Hill News.*

Valdés, G. (1995). The teaching of minority languages as academic subjects: Pedagogical and theoretical challenges. *Modern Language Journal, 79*(3), 299–328.

Yin, R. (1989). *Case study research: Design and methods.* Newbury Park, CA: Sage.

Background of the Project

This book was developed by the Center for Applied Linguistics (CAL) as part of a joint effort of two projects funded by the U.S. Department of Education: The National K–12 Foreign Language Survey Project and the Improving Foreign Language Education in Schools Project. The former was funded by the Office of Postsecondary Education, International Research and Studies Program, the latter by the Office of Educational Research and Improvement through a subcontract from the Northeast and Islands Regional Educational Laboratory At Brown University (LAB). The model programs effort was one component of each of the two projects.

Both projects have as a goal the identification of model programs leading to case studies that will provide educators with ideas and information on establishing and implementing early-start, long-sequence foreign language programs. The two projects joined forces to conduct a comprehensive and detailed study that would identify model programs in the northeast as well as other regions of the country.

Program Selection

Nearly a hundred programs were nominated, most of outstanding quality. The selection process was open to early-start, long-sequence programs that fit one of four models—FLES (foreign language in the elementary school), content-based FLES (referred to in this book as content-enriched FLES), immersion (partial, total, or two-way), or middle school continuation. Nominations were solicited nationally and submitted through a one-page nomination form distributed by foreign language professional organizations. Nominations from all educators were welcomed, but a particular effort was made to solicit suggestions from state and district foreign language supervisors.

The organizations and individuals that collaborated to publicize the nomination process included the American Association of Teachers of French (AATF), the American Association of Teachers of German (AATG), the American Association of Teachers of Spanish and Portuguese (AATSP), the American Council on the Teaching of Foreign Languages (ACTFL), the Center for Applied Linguistics (CAL), the National Association of District Supervisors of Foreign Languages (NADSFL), the National Council of State Supervisors of Foreign Languages (NCSSFL), the Northeast Conference on the Teaching of Foreign Languages (NEC), state representatives of the National Network for Early Language Learning (NNELL), and state liaisons of the Northeast and Islands Regional Educational Laboratory at Brown University (LAB). Each person who received a letter was asked to nominate one model program from their state.

The eligibility criteria outlined on the nomination form were based on current research on effective language instruction for elementary and middle school students (Curtain & Pesola, 1994; National Standards in Foreign Language Education Project, 1996) as well as on input from practitioners in the field. Nominated programs had to have the following characteristics:

- Curriculum based on the five Cs of the national foreign language standards (communication, cultures, connections, comparisons, and communities)
- Regular evaluation
- Outcomes that meet program goals

- Accessibility to all students
- Communication and coordination across content areas
- Ethnic and socioeconomic diversity reflective of the local student population
- Articulation from elementary through middle and high school
- At least 4 years of operation
- Willingness to share their curriculum
- Professional development opportunities
- Support from the community

Once the nominations were received, in January 1998, ineligible and incomplete entries were eliminated, and the remainder were sorted and reviewed in the following ways:

- Number of criteria met. The programs that met the highest number of the eligibility criteria listed above were identified.
- Geographic location. The goal was to select one program each from the west/southwest, southeast, mid-Atlantic, and midwest, and two from the northeast. A seventh program would be selected without regard to location.
- Program type. Each of the four program models—FLES, content-enriched FLES, immersion, and middle school continuation—needed to be represented by at least one of the programs selected. Two-way immersion programs were excluded, because there is more research available on them, and because model two-way programs have already been identified (see Loeb, 1999).
- Language(s) offered. An effort was made to ensure that the programs selected offered a variety of languages that are representative of those taught in U.S. schools.

The programs selected through these steps were then reviewed to make sure that programs from both district-wide and stand-alone schools were included and that selected programs included students from a range of socioeconomic levels and from urban magnet schools to middle-class suburban schools.

When the 90 nominated programs had been narrowed to 10 by the project researchers, the program selection panel met. This was a group of leaders in the field affiliated with the National Network for Early Language Learning (NNELL): Penny Armstrong, Audrey Heining-Boynton, and Marcia Rosenbusch. The final selection was reached by considering how well the programs met the 11 criteria (based on shared knowledge of the programs) and by ensuring that a variety of languages was represented.

Key staff of the seven selected programs agreed to (1) participate in a two-day site visit from project staff, (2) designate a school contact person to facilitate the site visit, (3) share their foreign language curriculum with others and submit it to the database of the Educational Resources Information Center (ERIC), and (4) allow other interested school personnel to visit their program.

Site Visits and Data Gathering

Data gathering included two-day visits by CAL project staff (Lucinda Branaman and Jennifer Locke) to each program in the spring of 1998 to gather as much information as possible. The extensive site visit protocols were based on data collection instruments used for case studies of language programs, including those used by Sheppard (1994) in a descriptive study of content–ESL practices. The case study design was selected as the method for gathering data on these programs, because it is "the preferred strategy when 'how' or 'why' questions are being posed, when the investigator has little control over events, and when the focus is on a contemporary phenomenon within some real-life context" (Yin, 1989, p.13).

The instruments were drafted by the project team in consultation with CAL staff who have expertise in qualitative data gathering in foreign language, bilingual, and ESL programs. Other preparations for the site visits included pilot testing and finalizing data-gathering instruments, finalizing classroom observation protocols, and making logistical arrangements with program staff. CAL staff activities at the sites included the following:

- Interviews with the school principal(s), district foreign language supervisor or school foreign language coordinator, foreign language teacher(s), regular classroom teacher(s), a student, a parent, and a school board representative.
- Classroom observations in six foreign language classes at different grade levels.
- Collection of written materials, including program philosophies and goals, curricula, lesson plans, class schedules, assessment instruments, student work, program evaluation reports and assessment outcomes, and public relations materials.

In addition to the data collected during the site visits, the project team at CAL contacted staff at the schools to supplement and correct all information to be published.

Materials From Pinellas County, Florida

Dear Parents,

Welcome to FLES (foreign language in the elementary school)! As a special part of our magnet school program, we are excited that each student (K-5) will receive twenty minutes of instruction in Spanish at least every other day. It is our hope to be able to offer a sequential program which begins with listening and speaking and later develops reading and writing skills, as well as cultural content.

The FLES program has been designed to give students the opportunity to hear only Spanish throughout a lesson which both teaches specific vocabulary and utilizes the classroom, and the many subjects taught there daily as a natural setting for the acquisition of a second language. Children will meet characters, such as "Vaca Lulú" and "Pancho", who speak only Spanish and will enjoy communicating with them through songs, stories and games. It is important to note that, at the early stages, it is natural for children to understand a lot more than they can say creatively on their own, just as it was when they acquired their native language. We emphasize also that language acquisition takes place only after a long sequence of study and reinforcement, and we urge you to have realistic expectations, keeping in mind that all children will be successful learners in FLES.

Although children will not receive a reportcard grade for Spanish, they will be evaluated regularly based on "culminating experiences". These experiences will provide the students with an opportunity to present to various segments of the school community samples of what they have learned. Presentations will be tied to specific language skills and will be documented and critiqued for the purpose of program evaluation.

Please look for the AMIGOS newsletter which will inform you of specifics of the FLES curriculum and will feature songs, poems and expressions for you to practice with your child at home.

Hasta pronto,
FLES Instructors:

FLES Song #1:

POLLITO, CHICKEN
Pollito, chicken
Gallina, hen
Lápiz, pencil y
Pluma, pen.
Ventana, window
Puerta, door
Mesa, table y
Piso, floor.
Azúcar, sugar
Amigo, friend
Maestra, teacher
Lo hiciste bien.

Pinellas County FLES Program Exit Rubric, Grade 5 (**DRAFT**)

I Can rubric - fifth grade

Parent Signature _____

Name _____   Teacher _____

School _____   #of years in FLES _____

I can.....in Spanish. (✔ = indicates at least 90% accuracy)

	Orally, or in conversation	In writing	Student	Peer	Teacher
1. name ten colors					
2. form number sentences, using addition, subtraction, multiplication and division, using numbers from 0 - ___					
3. express the current date and my birthdate correctly					
4. express the weather					
5. describe the clothing I am wearing					
6. describe the contents of my book bag					
7. describe my family with a minimum of five sentences					
8. read orally and comprehend a passage dealing the theme of with family					
9. express at least five things about my house					
10. read orally and comprehend a passage or real estate advertisement dealing with the house					

Pinellas County (Florida) FLES Team 1997

	Orally, or In conversation	In writing	Student	Peer	Teacher
11. list what I ate for breakfast, lunch and dinner					
12. describe my favorite foods/describe a well-balanced meal					
13. describe at least five of my favorite animals					
14. read orally and comprehend a story about animals					
15. name the continents in Spanish					
16. name the Spanish-speaking countries of Central America and their capitals					
17. name the Spanish-speaking countries of South America and their capitals					
18. name the planets					
19. narrate at least five facts about the planets					
20. talk about at least ten occupations that interest me					
21. read orally and comprehend a passage about people and what they do for a living					
22. name at least five modes of transportation					
23. describe at least five things I like to do					

I Can

ask and answer the following questions:

	Orally, or in conversation	In writing	Student	Peer	Teacher
24. ¿Cómo estás?					
25. ¿Cómo te llamas?					
26. ¿Cuántos años tienes?					
27. ¿De dónde eres?					
28. ¿Dónde vives?					
29. ¿Te gusta el español?					
30. ¿Juegas al _____?					

My class can

	date completed	comments
31. produce and follow simple instructions.		
32. describe people and products of Hispanic culture.		
33. ask and answer questions related to school.		
34. inquire about likes and dislikes of classmates and share results.		

	date completed	comments
35. use and interpret culturally appropriate gestures and oral expressions for greetings, leave-takings and classroom interactions.		
36. identify people and objects based on oral and written descriptors; provide short oral and written descriptions of common objects and people.		
37. retell the main theme and describe the characters of a book, poem or video presented in class.		
38. comprehend written messages on familiar topics.		
39. reproduce the main message and details of an advertisement (i.e. real estate).		
40. write a storyboard on a school event and broadcast it to the school.		
41. dramatize songs, stories and poetry for parents and community.		
42. plan and produce in groups a commercial on a topic related to the curriculum.		
43. use software containing stories and activities presented in class to practice Spanish.		

	date completed	comments
44. participate in a field trip designed to provide opportunities for interaction with the target culture (i.e. visit a Hispanic restaurant and order a meal in Spanish using an authentic menu).		
45. identify customs, holidays and patterns of behavior from the Hispanic culture as observed in literature, videos, field trips and through guest speakers.		
46. recognize age-appropriate cultural activities, such as games, songs and dances from the Spanish-speaking world.		
47. use Spanish to demonstrate concepts learned in the content areas, such as math, geography and language arts.		
48. use Spanish to participate in an activity, such as a science experiment, based on a concept being learned in the content class.		
49. cite and use examples of borrowed words and cognates from Spanish and English.		
50. contact through e-mail or letters a student or students living in South America or Spain.		

Pinellas County FLES Team/ 1997

Materials From Springfield Public Schools, Massachusetts

ELEMENTARY WORLD LANGUAGES LEARNING OUTCOMES

GRADE: 4   THEME: NUMBERS: GEOMETRY MEASUREMENT AND WORKING WITH DATA
LANGUAGE: ALL   NUMBER OF CLASSES:

CONTENT AREAS	OUTCOMES Students will. . .	VOCABULARY/ STRUCTURE	CULTURE	INSTRUCTIONAL ACTIVITIES	ASSESSMENT ACTIVITIES
MATH SCIENCE SOCIAL STUDIES GEO-GRAPHY	BE ABLE TO NAME THE DIFFERENT SHAPES BE ABLE TO MEASURE OBJECT USING A SIMPLE SHAPE	**CIRCLE SQUARE RECTANGLE** OVAL **DIAMOND CUBE PRISM CYLINDER CONE SPHERE TRIANGLE** MEASUREMENT LENGTH, (SHORTER LONGER) WIDTH,HEIGHT, WEIGHT GRAPH	SCIENCE AND MATH TERMS ARE UNIVERSAL AND THEREFORE EASY TO UNDERSTAND GRAPH DIF. RELIGION OR ETHNIC GROUPS OF A TARGET COUNTRY EXPOSURE TO THE MEDIA (NEWSPAPERS, MAGAZINES ETC. SHOW THAT MATH IS EVERYWHERE GRAPHING	USE TANGRAMS AND PATTERN BLOCKS TO CREATE OBJECTS USE MATH RELATED BOOKS IE: BOOK ABOUT SHAPES RELATE MEASUREMENT W / SCHOOL VOC. AND COLORS. MEASURE THE LENGTHS OF SIDES OF SHAPES IE: DESK GRAPHING	TEACHER OBSERVATION CLASS BOOK OR INDIVIDUAL BOOK OF SHAPES SHOW & TELL

LEARNING OUTCOMES

Subject: World Languages
STRAND Communication - Communicating in at least one language in addition to a first language.
LEVEL: K-2

OUTCOME: BY THE END OF K-2, students will develop comprehension and expression skills in a second language focused on the self and immediate surroundings.

PROGRESS INDICATORS:

Students will. .perform simple communicative tasks using single learned words and phrases, and learned expressions with no major repeated patterns of error to:

- Greet and respond to greetings.
- Introduce and respond to introductions.
- Describe, compare, and contrast.
- Ask and answer questions.
- Make and respond to requests.
- Express, verbally and/or nonverbally, likes, dislikes, and feelings.
- Express, verbally and/or nonverbally, needs.
- Express, verbally and/or nonverbally, agreement and disagreement.
- Follow directions.
- Provide and obtain information and knowledge.

CITY-WIDE OUTCOME ASSESSMENTS:

- Oral Interviews/ presentations, using visual prompts.
- Listening comprehension.
- Role plays.

Summary of
the Programs

Program	Program Type	Demographics	Profile
Bay Point Elementary School Pinellas County Public Schools, FL	• Spanish content-enriched FLES in a magnet school focusing on math, science, technology, and foreign language • curriculum based on the goals of the elementary school curriculum, incorporating the five Cs of the national foreign language standards	• urban school district with 106,687 students in 1997-98 • one of two magnet schools offering foreign language instruction to elementary students from the school attendance zone; other students from the district selected by lottery • school population of 689 students in 1997-98: 62% Caucasian, 33% African American, 2% Hispanic American, 2% Asian American • 33% of students qualify for free or reduced-price lunches	• 20-30 minutes a day of Spanish for all students in Grades K-5. • Spanish teachers travel from classroom to classroom with instructional materials carts • regular classroom teachers stay in the class for foreign language lessons
Springfield Public Schools Springfield, MA	• content-enriched FLES coordinated across subject areas, part of K-12 district-wide program • Spanish (all elementary schools) or French (Armory Street School and several others) starting in kindergarten; Russian and Chinese offered in a few elementary schools	• mid-sized urban school district with 26,000 students in 1997-98: 37% Hispanic, 31% Caucasian, 29% African American, 2% Asian • approximately 80% of students eligible for free or reduced-price lunch	• 30 minutes of foreign language instruction 3 times per week or 45 minutes twice per week in Grades 1-5 • 20-30 students per class
Ephesus Road Elementary School Chapel Hill-Carrboro City Schools Chapel Hill, NC	• French content-enriched FLES, part of district-wide K-12 language program • curriculum based on the goals of the elementary curricula, state foreign language guidelines, and the five Cs of the national standards	• large-town school district with 8,227 students in 1997-1998 • largest of seven elementary schools in district, which also includes three middle schools and two high schools • school population of 688 in 1997-98: 74% Caucasian, 15% African American, 9% Asian American, 2% Hispanic American • 14% of students qualify for free or reduced-price lunch	• 20 minutes of French instruction 4 days a week for all students in Grades 1-5 • about 25 students per class • teachers travel from classroom to classroom with instructional materials carts • regular classroom teachers often participate in the foreign language lessons • site-based management

Assessment	Articulation	Funding	Points of Interest
• outcome rubrics • portfolios • home assessment system involving parents, regular classroom teachers, and FLES teachers; students proceed at their own pace; results in a portfolio of students' foreign language performance	• continuation program at two middle schools; Spanish offered in high school	• federal magnet desegregation funding since 1993 • pilot program (1987-91) funded through State Foreign Language Elementary grant	• Café Olé, a stand-alone, realia-rich classroom and teacher office/materials room, used for technology-related classes, theatrical presentations and rehearsals, and Spanish Club meetings • teacher-produced Spanish language videos and Spanish song tapes
• district-wide listening comprehension assessment in Grade 3 • district-wide writing and speaking assessment in grades 8, 9, and 10 • state competency tests in Grades 4, 8, and 10 • trial versions of the state foreign language exam pilot tested in the spring of 2000	• articulated Grades K-12 in all languages • language teachers from all grade levels (K-12) meet regularly to ensure articulation and curriculum coordination • 6th-grade students choose from French, Spanish, or Chinese, continuing with language studied earlier or beginning new one • students in Grades 9-12 can choose to add Italian, Russian, German, or Latin	• foreign language teachers paid with funds from the district budget	• current language program re-organized in 1993; previous programs have operated since the 1950s • strong support from superintendent and the School Committee (similar to a board of education)
• fifth-grade end-of-year written assessment incorporating national standards, developed by district teachers • portfolios • student self-assessment of language skills	• students may continue with French at Middle School • advanced foreign language instruction offered at high school	• district funding, supplemented by assistance from the PTA and grants	• strong links to the University of North Carolina at Chapel Hill, especially the teacher training program • French program and student work featured on two Web sites

Program	Program Type	Demographics	Profile
Glastonbury Public Schools Glastonbury, CT	• Spanish content-enriched FLES in Grades 1-5, articulated with Grades 6-12 • in Grade 6, students choose whether to continue Spanish through Grade 12 or to start French and study it through Grade 12 • in Grade 7, students may add Russian • in high school, students may add Japanese or Latin	• middle-class suburb of Hartford, population 28,000 • 6,000 students attending five elementary schools, one sixth-grade school, one middle school, and one high school; one elementary magnet school shared with East Hartford, Connecticut • 88% of students Caucasian, 4% Hispanic, 4% Asian American, 3% African American • 6% of students qualify for free or reduced-price lunch	• 20 minutes of foreign language instruction two times per week in Grade 1 • 20 minutes per day in Grades 2-5 • 23 minutes per day in Grade 6 • 45 minutes per day in Grades 7-12 • about 21 students per class • separate school for sixth graders, The Academy School • interdisciplinary focus; foreign language curriculum topics parallel those presented in social studies, science, and language arts
Andrew Jackson Middle School and Greenbelt Middle School Prince George's County, MD	• partial French immersion magnet, continuation of a K-6 total immersion program, part of K-12 sequence • additional exploratory language and level I language study required of immersion students in Grades 7-8	• seventeenth largest school district in the nation • suburban school district adjacent to Washington, DC, with 126,515 students in 1997-98 • Greenbelt and Andrew Jackson are 2 of 26 middle schools (Grades 7-8) in the school district • 751 students at Greenbelt Middle School in 1997-98: 69% African American, 23% Caucasian, 4% Asian American, 3% Hispanic American; 36% eligible for free or reduced-price lunch • 625 students at Andrew Jackson Middle School in 1997-98: 83% African American, 9% Caucasian, 3% Hispanic American, 3% Asian American,1% Native American; 38% eligible for free or reduced-price lunch	• 26-30 students per class • two consecutive 50-minute periods per day taught in French: French language arts and world studies • interdisciplinary approach: students study and relate similar themes in social studies, English, language arts, and fine arts • admission to the K-12 program follows diversity and magnet guidelines; middle school program open to students with 6 years of French immersion at the elementary level • exploratory German, Japanese, Latin, Russian, Spanish, and Swahili (varies by school) required in Grade 7 • level 1 course in Japanese, Latin, Russian, or Spanish required in Grade 8

Assessment	Articulation	Funding	Points of Interest
• collaborative departmental examinations for Grades 5-12 focusing on all four language skills • portfolios to document student progress from elementary through high school • holistic exams • short-answer tests and quizzes (for grammar points) • oral proficiency interviews • presentations • authentic activities • self-assessment • program evaluation every 5 years	• Spanish taught in Grades 1-5. In Grade 6, students choose between French or Spanish to continue through Grade 12. In Grade 7, students may add Russian; in high school, they may add Japanese or Latin • collaboration between Glastonbury staff and the University of Connecticut to enhance articulation between high school and higher education	• district funding; additional funds from private, state, and federal government grants	• started in 1957, one of the longest running articulated programs in U.S. public schools • in Grades 7-12, 13%-15% of students studying two languages • parents given packets that help students new to the district transition into the program • for professional development, teachers are required to observe language teachers at other grade levels or to exchange classes across languages and grade levels
• authentic activities • creative writing samples and essays • traditional open-ended tests with a real-life focus • short-answer tests for grammatical concepts • class participation • oral assessment • student portfolios • classroom assessment results shared across grade levels and used to revise scope and sequence of the program each year • K-8 program evaluated by the Center for Applied Linguistics in July 1996	• French immersion and International Baccalaureate program courses at one high school	• district funding supplemented by magnet diversity funding	• numerous field trips and summer international trips as part of interdisciplinary curriculum • high retention rates: approximately 98% of students remain with the program from elementary to middle school

Program	Program Type	Demographics	Profile
Larchmont Elementary School Toledo Public Schools Toledo, OH	• content-enriched FLES Spanish pilot program, implemented in three district elementary schools, one each for Spanish, French, and German • instruction twice a week for 30 minutes for all students in Grades 1-6 • math, social studies, science, language arts/reading, music, health, and art reinforced through foreign language instruction	• urban school district with 39,667 students in 1997-1998: 51% Caucasian, 41% African American, 6% Hispanic American, 1% Asian American • 43 elementary schools in the district • neighborhood school with 319 students in 1997-1998: 86% Caucasian, 11% African American, 2% Hispanic American • 38% of students qualify for free or reduced-price lunch	• two 30-minute lessons, two times per week • teacher travels from classroom to classroom with instructional materials cart • most regular classroom teachers participate in the foreign language lesson • articulation forms completed by the classroom teacher to help the Spanish teacher coordinate language lessons with the curriculum content of the regular classroom
Richmond Elementary School Portland Public Schools Portland, OR	• Japanese partial immersion in Grades K-5 • part of projected K-12 sequence begun in 1989, one grade added each year • city-wide magnet school	• magnet program population representative of Portland ethnic demographics: 67% Caucasian, 16% Asian American, 10% African American, 5% Hispanic American, 2% Native American • 563 students at Richmond Elementary School; 330 students in magnet program, drawn from all over the city • 24% of Richmond students qualify for free or reduced-price lunch	• two classes of 25-28 students in each grade • Japanese teachers have an English-speaking counterpart at each grade with whom they plan and coordinate integrated thematic instruction • all subjects except English language arts taught in both Japanese and English, including geography, health, art, science, literature, government, math, and history (emphasis varies by grade level) • separate classrooms for Japanese and English language teachers with culturally appropriate materials • holistic approach to language acquisition in which listening, speaking, reading, and writing are integrated • learning centers, books, creative play objects, art supplies, and at least two computers in each classroom

Assessment	Articulation	Funding	Points of Interest
• informal assessment on a regular basis • student portfolios in Grades 2-6 • end-of-year formal assessments in Grades 4-6	• middle school continuation program has been discontinued • Spanish offered for seventh graders at district's central International Studies Center	• district funding for curriculum development and salaries • district and school funding for instructional supplies	• strong district, school, and parent support • centralized International Studies Center enhances assessment and articulation efforts • creative incentive programs to encourage student participation in class
• state assessment in Japanese (still under development for lower grades) • work sample collection for all subjects for every academic year, including scored writing samples in both Japanese and English • videotaped annual oral interview assessments following state benchmarks	• Richmond program links to Grades 6-8 at Mount Tabor Middle School, which links to program at Grant High School • one additional grade added to program each year, reaching Grade 12 in 2001-2002	• regular district funding and district magnet funding • additional funds from private and government grants • additional funds from Oya No Kai, a parent group, for materials, trips, and international homestays	• extensive program support organization, including a non-profit Japanese immersion foundation, formed by parents • cultural exchange trip to Japan for students in Grade 5 • exposure to Japanese writing beginning in kindergarten • Japanese interns and volunteers assist teachers in the classroom • two Japanese immersion camps each summer

Program Contact Information

Bay Point Magnet Elementary
Gaye Lively, Principal
62nd Avenue South
St. Petersburg FL 33712
Tel: 727-893-2398
E-mail: PinFLES@aol.com
Web sites—
    http://members.aol.com/jschw6/FLES-mainpage.html.
    http://www.geocities.com/Athens/Acropolis/8714

Springfield Public Schools
Dr. Kathleen Riordan, Foreign Language Director
195 State Street
P.O. Box 1410
Springfield MA 01102-1410
Tel: 413-787-7111
Fax 413-787-6713
E-mail: riordank@springfield.ma.us

Ephesus Road Elementary School
Carol Orringer, French Teacher
1495 Ephesus Church Road
Chapel Hill NC 27514
Tel: 919-929-8715
Fax: 919-969-2366
E-mail: corringer@chccs.k12.nc.us
Web sites—
    http://www.sunsite.unc.edu/-ephesus
    http://www.media-international.net/ethno

Glastonbury Public Schools
Christine Brown, Director of Foreign Languages
232 Williams Street
Glastonbury CT 06033
Tel: 860-652-7954
Fax: 860-652-7978
E-mail: cbrownglas@aol.com

Prince George's County Public Schools
Dr. Pat Barr-Harrison, Foreign Language Supervisor
9201 East Hampton Drive
Capitol Heights MD 20743-3812
Tel: 301-808-8265 ext 227
Fax: 301-808-8291
E-mail: pbarr@pgcps.org

Larchmont Elementary School
Jeffrey Hanthorn, Principal
Maria Martínez, Spanish Teacher
1515 Slater Street
Toledo OH 43612
Tel: 419-476-3787
Fax: 419-470-6552
E-mail: j.hanthorn@tps.org

Richmond Elementary School
Deanne Balzer, Resource Teacher
Japanese Magnet Program
Rebecca McWaters, Principal
2276 SE 41st Avenue
Portland OR 97214
Tel: 503-916-6220
Fax: 503-916-2665
E-mail: dbalzer@pps.k12.or.us
Web sites—
    http://www.oyanokai.org
    http://www.moshihola.org